To Live and Drink in L.A.

by

Ben Peller

ALGONQUIN ROUND TABLE PUBLISHING

Cover Photo by Jill Demby Guest
Rear photos by Nian Aster and Jill Demby Guest

Published by Algonquin Round Table Publishing

ISBN: 0615436366
ISBN-13: 9780615436364

To my Grandfather, Edward S. Michals,
For being the kind of man I hope
to one day grow into becoming

And to all who have opened this
book and chosen to embrace life
with a wink and a smile
(and perhaps a cocktail)

ACKNOWLEDGMENTS

To my Aunts and Uncles, for believing in me long after I'd stopped believing in myself

To all my cousins, for inspiring me through pursuit of their own dreams

This book wouldn't have come about without me encountering all the characters I've met in Los Angeles... Scott, Patricia, Mandy, Tony, Dominic, Valter, Carl, Priscilla, Jim, Victoria, Todd, Grand, Theresa, Isla, Bill (B.J.), Christine, Bob, Lili, Marta, Lisa, Hilary, Alex, Stephanie, Jason, Diane, Cynthia, Mark, Simone, Edgar, Derek... Good Lord, if I missed you, I promise to give you a shout-out in the next book

To Richard, for being one of the strongest and bravest men I know

My thanks to Elizabeth for believing in spilling blood on the page

To Bambi, for being a dear

Cheers go out to Jill, who's dropped me off and picked me up at the Jim-Jam Clinic on more than one occasion.

To Viva, for reasons that need not be explained here

A special kudos to Justin, for remembering the "Big Guns" t-shirt

Much thanks to Team Fusion, for their untiring support and unrelenting awesomeness

To Christopher James Defoor, a lifelong friend and one who knows a good session when he has one

Thank you, Dr. John Schultheiss, for introducing to me the possibility of controlling my own existence

A bow to Max Brooks, for not only warning us all about the upcoming battle, but for providing me with the inspiration for the final page of this book

And, finally, thank you Marvin, for always asking me how the writing was going – Bless you, my friend – it's going good.

"The Bar. Sure. It overlooked the takeoff ramp."

– Charles Bukowski
"Tales of Ordinary Madness"

"Naked. I was drunk and naked for all the world to see.
It was a sobering thought that continued to haunt me…"

– David Sedaris
"Naked"

*To the best of my knowledge this is a work of fiction,
but knowing the protagonist and the city involved…
well, anything is possible.*

TABLE OF CONTENTS

PREFACE

Before you put this down, please let me explain.

I knew the protagonist of this work, Shawn Michals (NOT to be confused with *, whose gimmicked name is owned by the *[1]), only briefly. We were both professional wrestlers back in the day. We spent more afternoons and evenings than I care to remember in the back of vans and in hotel rooms, trying to ignore the other's incessant snore and occasional flatulence.

Even back then Shawn was something of an enigma. The closest he ever came to revealing anything about his past was that his grandfather's original name had been "Michalski." Upon arriving from Poland the admitting officers at Ellis Island had changed "Michalski" to the more pronounceable "Michals." That was the reason, Shawn stated, that his last name was spelled "Michals" and not "Michaels."

"Everyone always thinks it's because Polacks can't spell," he told me once, grinning. "Why is it everyone doesn't usually know a damn thing?"

"Because they don't care enough to find out," I proposed.

---

1   Names deleted at insistence of publisher's lawyers.

Shawn's smile exploded into a laugh as he cocked an eyebrow in my direction. He had a way of staring at you that was pretty flattering. As if whatever you'd just said was something he ought to memorize. "You mind if I use that?" he asked.

"Use it?" I asked. "Use it for what?"

He took a liberal swallow from the clear green bottle in his hand. "I'm a writer," he said. "I'm always on the lookout for people with a story to tell. You seem like you've got a few. Do you?"

Did I? It seemed like a challenge. I tugged at my tank top awkwardly and stammered, "I have no idea."

Shawn just sat back, had another sip of his concoction, and smiled. "That's why you should be a writer," he said. I could smell the vodka seeping from his breath. "Good writers never have any inherent faith in their stories. They have to draw them out of themselves, like a weapon against that blank space in front of them. Spill blood on the page."

Blood on the page. Shawn often popped off quotes such as this. In a way he frightened me. There was a certain intensity he carried, as though he were a bomb about to go off. Not to mention he seemed to be drunk, or at least buzzed, most of the time. Never quarrelsome, but never sober either. When I asked him what he did for a living he just laughed. "I live," he replied.

In time I would decide that being a pro wrestler was not my destiny. I proceeded to settle down with my life, and found a wonderful woman and had a child who I've never regarded as anything less than a miracle. I halfheartedly followed Shawn's career as a wrestler. He had a very successful and very brief run in the largest pro wrestling organization in the world. Occasionally I found myself envying him, but then I would stare into the eyes of my daughter and not regret a thing.

Then came the day I got the phone call.

It was from the manager of an apartment complex in West Los Angeles. Shawn hadn't paid his rent in two months, and eviction proceedings were underway. Apparently he had listed me as an "emergency contact." Why, I couldn't fathom. But I dutifully went to the building and accepted the key to Shawn's apartment from the manager. I unlocked the door and ventured inside figuring I would find an address book, a phone with saved numbers, or at least some kind of connection to another entity who might be able to explain his whereabouts.

What I found was chaos. It was a studio apartment, and there was no bed, no pictures of relatives, no indication that whoever lived here had a past of any kind. Neither was there a telephone, a computer, a television, or any evidence at all that he was in contact with the outside world. But there were books. You couldn't put your foot down without stepping on one. Along with these books were pieces of paper, napkins, and paper bags, all strewn with words. Pens littered the landscape like spent bullet cartridges. The smell was, to be charitable, rustic. Vodka bottles occupied the kitchen floor, lined up in a semi-strategic pyramid that stretched from the far wall to the entranceway of the living room/bedroom area. I was only barely able to open the refrigerator door, and once I did found it empty anyway.

I made my way out of the kitchen, but one of the napkins stuck to the bottom of my shoe. I reached down, yanked it off, and stared at it. It was a cocktail napkin from the Loews Hotel in Santa Monica. I started to read the words upon it, their letters neat but so small as to present a challenge of sorts. I sat down and kept reading.

Real Novelty dances on
the edge of chaos

- God's laughing. Somewhere,
- Is that right?
- Sure. He gave you life. And
  you're still alive, aren't you?
- Yes.
- Then don't you feel you should
  do something about it? (beat)
  If only to give him a punchline?

:)
                    —Loews Hotel
                  Santa Monica
                      Summertime

When I finished that napkin I reached down
and picked up a paper bag from Ralph's. I
read the words on that makeshift canvas,
and then snatched up a third page, this
one a sheet of yellow notebook paper. I
read. And read.

I spent the next two weeks reading.

Gradually the different haphazard
scrolls began to form a cohesive order of
sorts. Some were even titled. As I began to
see a certain pattern to these seemingly

wild writings, I recalled a conversation I'd had with Shawn after our first and only match together. It had been a fun bout, and afterwards in the locker room we shared a beer and spoke about hopes and dreams. He predicted he was going to die young, and I asked him what he wanted on his tombstone.

He stared back at me. The trace of a smile on his lips; his expression was the one I always searched for whenever I looked in the mirror. "He lived," he announced. "Put that on my tombstone. He *lived.* How many people can honestly say that?"

I was at a loss for an answer. That was the night I decided to quit wrestling and enter a new chapter in my life. I never saw Shawn Michals again.

But to this day I feel maybe because when he made this confession to me and I actually seemed to listen is the reason he put me down as someone to contact in the case of an emergency.

Be forewarned: these stories aren't so much about drinking as they are about living. Yes, Shawn liked his drink. He also liked his life.

I've attempted to put these stories in some sort of chronological order but in the words of Harold Pinter, Shawn's life was not, in keeping with the state of his apartment, "so neat and tidy." Within these pages you will find gaps, time jumps, and also a few authentic stills of drawings and scribblings. As with the case of the previously pictured napkin, I felt there were certain artifacts of Shawn's life in Los Angeles that were, as he himself might put it, best bled directly onto the page.

Perhaps I may go visit him someday. I believe I know where he is, and after reading this book, you'll have your ideas about where he is as well. But in the meantime, I prefer to leave him in the peace he's apparently found. There is little peace in these writings. In them you will find a man caught between ages. In this time when creativity has taken a backseat to reality, the renaissance era this is not. Shawn Michals was the kind of man who grew ill at the use of "LOL" and "OMG." Some would argue that he was nothing more than a wastrel, but others would propose that he was deeply sensitive, and his seemingly constant intoxication was a shield against a world falling out of love with the written word.

Many different people move to Los Angeles, California for many different reasons. The usual suspect is that people want to be in "the industry." Fledging actors, directors, makeup artists, caterers… they all flock here, drawn by the **HOL-LYWOOD** sign and a climate that promises wondrous sunsets over an ocean framed by palm trees.

However, there are other reasons people head west. Some are in search of a father figure, some are tracking down their dream of becoming a professional wrestler, and others are crazy enough to want to become writers in the city of Angels. Also, as they say, "You don't have to shovel sunshine. And there's always a perfect sunset around the corner."

Shawn was a man who, though some would consider completely out of his mind, never stopped searching for that perfect sunset, the one that doesn't glow too intently or linger for too long. Perhaps as you traverse these seemingly disjointed pieces of the puzzle that chronicle Shawn Michals' time in L.A., you'll catch glimpses of a perfect sunset of your own. One that knows when the time is right to sink beneath the ocean, and move on to the next day.

Some may say his writings glamorize a life of dissipation. Still more may point to questionable moral values. For better or worse it is indisputable that within these pages Shawn, true to his wish *lives.*

But take it from me; he may take some getting used to. I speak from experience.

- B.P.

THE LIZARD KING'S LEATHER PANTS

I grew up in the Midwest, raised on a steady musical diet of Simon and Garfunkel, John Denver, and a host of other folk and country artists (my mother was a great believer in the theories that rock music had a drumbeat that counteracted one's heartbeat, not to mention that if you played Led Zeppelin's "Stairway to Heaven" backwards you could hear the words *Sweet Satan*). This paranoid nature of life's wilder sides extended to her view of alcohol, which she described as "the Devil's Brew," claiming it had ruined just about every male in our family with the exception of my alleged birth father, who managed to be a bitter abusive man without ever having taken a drink in his life.

Thus, when I first moved to L.A. my knowledge of both rock music and drinking was horribly deficient. This changed in short order. I started hanging out on the Sunset Strip, particularly at the Rainbow Bar and Grill, where drinks were strong enough to make even seasoned alcoholics gladly pay the two drink minimum it cost to get into the club.

The Rainbow is where I was first introduced to the legend that is Jim Morrison. I was standing at the bar, trying to look cool in my strategically torn jeans and muscle shirt, when a goateed gentlemen walked by, stopped and did a double take. "Jim!" he exclaimed.

"Say wha'?" I replied. I was on my third drink.

"As I live and breathe, you look just like my man Jim!"

The following exchange is blurred in my recollection, but the gist of it is that the man at first expressed disbelief and then outright anger that I was unfamiliar with Jim Morrison, who he referred to as "the poet laureate of fuckin' rock n' roll." At the time, I wasn't yet a poet. I sure as hell was nowhere near a rock star. But I had plans to become both, and I was already learning to love drinking. That and my long hair apparently made me a potential successor to Jim's throne, at least in my new friend's eyes.

"Leather pants," he trumpeted. "A pair of leather pants and you'd look just like the Lizard King!"

"The Lizard King…" I mused, ordering another train-misser. "So what made Jim Morrison the Lizard King?"

"When he was a child, he saw a Native American die and felt as though this dying man's spirit entered his body. He wrote a poem in which he proclaimed himself the Lizard King. He created, more or less, himself. Plus, he was a rock star who wrote poetry, got laid left and right, and drank himself to death."

I spent the rest of the night introducing myself to women as Jim Morrison's illegitimate son. Unfortunately such a declaration required proof, and I was questioned as follows:

Where did your "father" die?

What was your "father's" middle name?

Why are you trying to bite on Jim Morrison's reputation, you pathetic poseur?

Finally a vision of teased blonde hair wearing a short jean skirt and a black halter top responded to my stubborn declaration of being Jim Morrison's offspring with, "Really? That's awesome!" As we started making out her hand slipped around to my butt.

As soon as her fingers grazed my ass she jerked back abruptly. "Where the hell are your leather pants?" she asked.

Clearly the situation regarding my birthright needed remedying.

My Aunt Carrie has a successful leather apparel business up in Northern California. She's a wonderful person, opens her home up to any stray cats that may be wandering about, and is a teetotaler. Oddly, we get along wonderfully.

However, when she asked me what I wanted for my birthday that year and I replied I would love a pair of leather pants, there was a lengthy pause. "Leather pants?" she asked.

"Yeah, you know. Like Jim Morrison had."

"Huh," she said. Carrie's *huhs* are rich enough to claim their own adjectives. There's the contemplative "huh," the disgruntled "huh," the amazed "huh." And so forth.

This "huh" was along the lines of *Well, I guess Shawn's finally come out.*

Trooper that Carrie is, she promised to work on them. And then, a month later, they arrived. They were brilliant. They fit great, and I was surprised and delighted that in addition to making me look semi-rebellious they had the added bonus of making it appear as though I had the semblance of an ass.

It didn't take me too long to make an ass out of myself while wearing them. Now that I wore leather pants, ala Jim Morrison, I felt it was my duty to write poems. I filled up notebooks with poems boasting titles such as "Suspended," "Bottom of my Fourth Bottle," and "Hungover Inutero." Most of these odes to drinking are now lost, but I'm sure parts of them live on in infamy in the minds of the hapless patrons I terrorized at neighborhood watering holes on Karaoke nights. Fortified by drink, I would pick Lynyrd Skynyrd's "Freebird," and instead of singing along would recite one of my lost poems while the haunting music played in the background. I even tried to expose myself one night in a place called, appropriately, The Bare Inn. I suppose I was trying to emulate Morrison's performance in Miami. However, L.A. isn't Miami, I wasn't Jim, and the incident didn't propel me into immortal infamy. Instead all it got me was a visit from the main security guard, a large man with spiky hair and tattoos running up and down his arms, who hauled me off the stage as I continued to rant my poem. "See 'ya, Jim," he chuckled as he guided me out the rear doorway usually reserved for deliveries.

The next morning, I told myself that being called "Jim" had made the incident worthwhile.

Hungry for more, I continued my rounds. I also started to read up on Jim Morrison in an attempt to discover what kind of person he was, or at least what kind of person others thought he was. The more I read about his apparent craziness, his rebellion, his search… the more I found I could relate. I'd come out to Los Angeles both running from something and searching for something, but neither was concrete in my mind. They both were as elusive as the soul of L.A. itself. Many people in this town seemed to be looking for something to grasp on to, whether it be acting, writing, directing, or simply being able to brag about lying on a sun drenched beach in the middle of January. As Morrison himself wrote ala *L.A. Woman*, "Well, I just got into town about an hour ago. Took a look around, see which way the wind blows..."

There is that peculiar sense about L.A., that hot winds like the Santa Anas can spark fire anywhere, the letters of the **HOLLYWOOD** icon can make mere mortals grow into people forty feet tall looming over Sunset Boulevard. An insecure kid from anywhere can become a God or Goddess. Or a King.

This aimless chutzpah of Los Angeles was infecting me, and in that vein my leather pants became a sort of teleportation device. Putting them on, I felt myself slipping into the spirit of the Lizard King. Though this was no doubt a mental journey of my own design, the results were concrete enough: I found myself drinking with Morrison's abandon, and I also seemed to be possessed with a touch of disparate genius. One night I regaled a bar with a monologue from *The Iceman Cometh,* in which one of the lead characters confesses to killing his wife. Another night I was able to stun the patrons of the Saddleback Ranch with a retelling of the legend of the formation of the Doors, acting out the scene from Oliver Stone's movie. I even sang "Moonlight Drive," and when everyone at the bar applauded, I bowed and started on "Roadhouse Blues." I was midway through the number when the head security guy (who also had tattoos up and down his arms) came over and mercifully put me out of everyone's misery.

There I stood on Sunset Boulevard, wondering when the next bus was due to come along, when I was approached by a woman with multicolored hair and a mischievous smile.

"Were you serious about what you said in there?" this mystery girl asked me.

"Of course," I said, having no idea what I'd said in there.

"You're really Jim Morrison's illegitimate son?" she asked. "And those are really a pair of his pants you're wearing."

She said this as if she didn't believe it, but was willing to for the sake of argument. I regarded her more closely, admiring her shoulder length hair that ran the spectrum from Red to Violet, encompassing all the colors of a rainbow. It angled loosely down to the small of her back, framing her face as though she were a pot of gold. She seemed to be chewing suggestively on something and was swaying just a bit. My kind of girl.

I slapped my magical leathers. "Absolutely," I drawled.

"Where are you going?" she asked.

I shrugged. "Home, I guess."

"How are you getting there?" she smiled. "You're not driving, I hope."

I assured her I hadn't driven in a year and a half and wasn't about to stop a good thing now.

"Do you need a ride?" she suggested. "Or anything?"

The problem with scoping out potential serial killers in Los Angeles is that many serial killers are charming and have a flair for the dramatic. While not everyone in L.A. is charming, almost all tend towards the dramatic. This potential lover/killer was no exception. She proceeded to whisper in my ear that she often believed she was the female Jim Morrison, and it was her destiny to find his spiritual entity in this dimension so that she could come together with him, thus reuniting their masculine and feminine energies in a supernova of timeless kinesis.

Out of all that, what I caught was "come together."

What would the Lizard King do?

Twenty minutes later, we were at my apartment passing a small pipe back and forth. Her name was Cynthia, and she was a songwriter. It was her sixth month in

L.A., but already from playing around town she had 1,867 friends on her Facebook page.

"One thousand, eight hundred and sixty-seven friends?" I pondered aloud, unable to comprehend meeting so many people in one lifetime, much less making friends with all of them. "That doesn't sound possible."

"They're not really friends. They're just people who, you know, friend me as someone to know."

"Huh," I said. "How many real friends do you have?"

She shrugged. "I'm not sure."

"Me neither."

"You're not really Jim Morrison's kid, are you?" she asked. Her tone had changed; no longer an alluring temptress, she seemed sad, sympathetic. Maybe she really was one of my spiritual entities; another wandering soul who sometimes felt a prisoner of her own dreams.

"Cynthia," I told her quietly. "All I can say is, I believe I could be. We all have the power to create ourselves, right? That's part of what makes us human, isn't it?"

I prayed I was sounding profound. With the marijuana and cocktails doing battle with one another within me I realized just how beautiful this woman was, and how much I wanted to make this night one to remember.

As if reading my mind, Cynthia reached over and began running her hand up my thigh. "How about we get those leather pants off of you so you can breathe, Jim junior?" she purred.

Drunk and stoned, I was in no shape to protest.

A shotgun blast of consciousness ambushed me. My first move, honed by years of experience, was automatic: check to make sure my wallet and credit cards were still in my pockets.

I discovered I was clad only in my boxers. Fair enough. Things had gotten pretty amorous last night, obviously. I looked around. Cynthia was nowhere to be seen. Well, I wasn't in a bathtub packed with ice and a note saying to call 911. This was a good thing.

Quickly I scanned my room. Nothing appeared out of place. My stuffed animal, Schmoo-Schmoo, was wedged against the edge of the bed and the wall, his usual place whenever I entertained a sleepover partner. Papers were still strewn by the rocking chair in front of my electric word processor. The puke green bureau I'd salvaged from a yard sale for five dollars still supported my stereo, CDs, loose change, and an heirloom watch my grand-

father had given me. The walls were still
adorned with the covers of pro wrestling
magazines and Playboys, lending what one
of my buddies had termed a "bisexual edge"
to my living abode.

As far as I could tell nothing had been
touched.

Except, hopefully, Cynthia and me.

But I couldn't remember. What had we
gotten up to last night? I rolled out of
bed and dropped to the floor in my prayer
position. I performed my morning prayer
of giving thanks for life, which I've
credited with, amongst other things, my
seeming immunity to hangovers.

I rose, intending to head to the freezer
and pour a cocktail to celebrate yet another evening too wild to remember. But
then decided I really ought to locate my
leather pants first.

I took inventory again. Shirts and shorts
were hanging from door handles and the
edge of the closet door. My Chicago Cubs
hat was perched above a wooden mushroom.
Even a pair of women's panties I'd been
meaning to take down for weeks was dangling familiarly from their post atop the
cracked mirror that hung from the center
wall.

But no leather pants.

The phone rang and I snapped it up
quickly, half hoping it was my guest from

last night calling to explain the where-abouts of my beloved trousers.

"Hello?"

It was a friend of mine, Tony. A fellow bar aficionado with a penchant for yelling "Oooooleander" whenever he entered a watering hole and then proceeding to order "Page six" when asked what he wanted to drink.

"How are you, brother?" he asked. "Any action last night?"

"I think so," I replied, feeling around my boxers. Dry. I leaned down and sniffed. Nothing.

"What was his name?" Tony laughed.

Phone in hand, I stalked from my studio into the kitchen. Cracked stove, toaster oven that managed to burn every damn piece of bread I ever put in there, and my army of empty 1.75 liter bottles of Smirnoff bottles on the floor, all stacked up like good soldiers. I'd been placing them there for the past couple months, claiming them as an art project of sorts. Truth was, I'd been saving them to prove to myself that I wasn't drinking that much. The only glitch was, after about four months, there were thirty-three of them nestled on the floor and it was making it difficult to maneuver around the cramped space.

I jerked open the fridge. A container of fat-free Velveeta slices, a bottle of

Diet Mountain Dew, and assorted ketchup and teriyaki sauce pouches. But no leather pants.

"Where the hell are they?" I shouted into the phone.

"They?" Tony crooned. "Wow, you must've had yourself a time last night."

"Tones, I love you," I said as I padded back into my studio. "But I'm going through a bit of a crisis right now. I may have to call you back."

"Is this an ooleander type of story?" This was Tony's term for a story that was preferably told in a bar.

"I can't find my leather pants!"

There was a respectful silence, followed by a long whistle. "Hey, man." Tony said. "I'm sorry. They get your keys and everything?"

"Fuck my keys!" I snapped as I took my search into the bathroom. "I loved those pants!"

My bathroom stared back mournfully at me. Toothpaste stains in the sink and a flimsy shower curtain, which I pulled back dramatically, hoping against hope to discover a pair of leather pants tied to the showerhead.

But there was nothing except a tub no discerning person would ever set foot in. I slowly slid the shower curtain back and wandered back out to my bed, where I collapsed.

"I need a drink," I told Tony.

"I'll be over in twenty minutes."

About two hours later, Tony and I were at Baja Cantina in Venice, and the Cantina's smooth but vigorous margaritas along with my self-forgiving mind had blurred last evening's episode into one to be proud of. No longer had it been a night in which after I passed out drunk my leather pants, my credit cards, and my keys were stolen by a woman with hair that belonged on a parakeet. No. Instead it became an evening of ravenous sex and thunderous orgasms. Obviously, I concluded to Tony after my fourth margarita, she'd taken my leather pants as a souvenir. A trophy, if you will.

"She's probably having them bronzed as we speak," Tony smiled, signaling for another round to cement my fantasy.

Who says one can't find any true friends in L.A.?

When I called the credit card companies to cancel the cards, I learned none of them had been used. This only compounded the mystery. That thieving vixen hadn't even used one of the credit cards to buy gas on her way home as I slept! What kind of amateur criminal was she?

To make matters more embarrassing, I didn't even have one of her business cards. I didn't know her last name. Hence I couldn't stalk her on Facebook and demand to know the whereabouts of my leathers.

Over the next few weeks, I remained halfway convinced my inexplicable visitor had stashed those leather pants somewhere under my nose. I continued to explore areas of my apartment I hadn't checked in months. From the pullout drawer under the oven to the closet in the kitchen that was supposed to house cleaning supplies, I scoured my apartment. No leather pants.

There was no way I could reveal the truth to my Aunt Carrie, so I made up a story about "outgrowing" the leather pants and donating them to a silent auction that would benefit the homeless.

Her "Huh" sounded like a relieved one, but then she followed it with a disbelieving one, and then came her question as to who would possibly bid on a pair of used leather pants.

"This *is* L.A.," I replied, offering my standard response to any question asked by family members when the real answer might cause embarrassment.

So I bought a new pair of leather pants from The Gap, stopped reading poetry at Karaoke nights, acknowledged that Jim Morrison was but one in a line of many men I'd claimed as a "real father," and considered the matter closed.

ॐ ॐ ॐ

Almost a year after I'd finally accepted that the disappearance of my leather pants was one of those grand mysteries life occasionally throws at us, one that's never meant to be solved, I was leafing through an entertainment magazine and came across an interview with a musician. She was a self-professed "rock grrrrl." Her face was vaguely familiar, but it was her rainbow colored hair that truly brought back that fateful night. Her photo showed her wearing a pair of familiar leather pants and a tank top, scowling seductively with a microphone in one hand and a bottle of Jack Daniels in the other.

I scanned the interview and got to a quote that I could hear her murmur in that seductive husky tone she'd used on me: "I like to consider myself the feminine incarnation of Jim Morrison. I even have a pair of his pants. This guy I had a one night stand with gave them to me. Of course, I don't know if they're really Morrison's pants. But this guy seemed to really believe it, you know? So when he told me he was Morrison's illegitimate kid, who knows? And when I wear the pants, I sometimes feel like Morrison's spirit is inside of me, you know?"

I looked up from the magazine, proud that she could mistake my spirit for Jim Morrison's. Could it be that I was correct in thinking I had a touch of Morrison in me? A quiet soft-spoken guy who became wild as hell when drunk, a young man who was alienated from his father, an artist who seemed to crave both solitude and adulation, there was much about him I could relate to. Morrison also believed, in his art, his words, in his testing of boundaries. And if in the end he began to believe too much in the "Lizard King" myth he created, perhaps that was an inevitability. In a land that can breed illusions as rampantly as Los Angeles, sometimes you need belief. Belief that you belong, belief that you're worthy and that your path is a notable one. It's this faith that can blaze through reality and forge a shelter from the storm of passing years. In L.A., as in life, it's best to make only the moment matter. For the moment is our only present, our only home, one that is us, all our own.

Just make sure to keep on your pants.

STRANGE LOVE:
HOW PRO WRESTLING HELPED ME
LEARN TO RELAX AND LOVE MY MOM

Just two months after my eighteenth birthday a miraculous event occurred. After a lifelong struggle with manic-depression, my mother committed suicide.

Her name was Jane Michals, and she was not just bipolar but stealthy to boot, for I was the only one she confessed her plans to. "I'm going to finish what I started with you," she would often tell me, after swearing me to secrecy. "And then I'm going to take myself away from this moronic dimension."

With the man who'd allegedly impregnated my mother long since out of the picture, Mom had raised me alone. This made her my constant companion, and guilt followed with her. In part because she constantly bemoaned the fact that I'd been born and that she had to raise a son by herself, but mostly what she made me feel bad about was keeping her from her self appointed date with destiny.

People who are bipolar sometimes find themselves gifted with extraordinary artistic abilities such as writing immortal poetry or creating revolutionary paintings. My mom was blessed, but her talent manifested itself in a more physical sense. She possessed a wicked right arm, and I learned to duck at an early age. Lamps, ashtrays, portable televisions… anything that wasn't nailed down became a potential projectile when Mom was in one of her "lithium-free" periods. If she'd been a male she might've been a pitcher in the major leagues. Unfortunately her chromosomes made this impossible. So it seemed from the time I was very young we forged an unspoken pact… she would throw, I would duck… and we'd ride out my growing up and see what happened.

When on lithium Mom would stay in her bedroom for days at a time. As I walked past on my way to school or a friend's house, I'd sometimes catch her peeking out of the door. It would shut quickly as I passed. "Don't worry," I'd call out. "Everything's okay."

These periods of peace were always pleasant. Also entertaining were the first few months after she'd go off lithium. She'd turn into a fireball of energy, applying for three different jobs at once and a full load of classes at the community college. Throughout my childhood into adolescence, my mother worked a smorgasbord of jobs that included a forest ranger, a museum tour guide, a substitute teacher, and an assistant to a world-renowned astrologist at North-western University. Amazingly charming in interviews and for the first couple months on the job, eventually Mom's rest-lessness, aided by lack of lithium, got the better of her and she became too much to handle. She was usually fired for inci-dents that involved projectiles.

Though I sometimes wished I could fire her as my mother, life with her was cer-tainly not dull. She claimed to be able to see new constellations in the sky, and took me on field trips to gang-infested neighborhoods as well as art galleries. "Life is but a dream, Shawn." She would always tell me. "And a dream is whatever you want to make it. Remember that." Then she would begin to hum *Merrily Merrily Merrily Merrily, Life is but a dream…,* and she wouldn't stop until I joined in with her.

These were the times when I thought I might be one of the luckiest kids alive.

After all, I did have my own share of eccentricities, such as conducting mara-thon pro wrestling sessions with a fat pillow in my bedroom. Mom would pass by my room and instead of asking me what the hell I, a fifteen year old kid was doing throwing a pillow around, she would sim-ply laugh and yell, "Go Champ!"

By the time I was seventeen I'd liber-ated a high jump mat from my high school and took to staging matches with imaginary opponents in the front yard. One afternoon I scrounged up the guts to climb to the roof of the house and look down at my phantom adversary sprawled helplessly on the mat twenty feet below. As I stood there wondering if I'd be able to clear the flower garden, I heard a voice.

"Jump!"

It was my mother, standing on the front porch wearing a smock and holding a spoon dripping with wet clay.

I hesitated, frightened by visions of myself missing the mat and landing in the red petunias and dirt.

"*Jump,* you fucker!" Mom shouted.

I glared over at her, and just to show her I wasn't about to be intimidated, I climbed down from the roof and took a few steps over to the mat and performed a routine elbow drop.

When I looked up, she'd gone back into the house.

During my senior year, the high school guidance counselor called my house after I'd told him in a career counseling session that I intended to become a pro wrestler.

"Yeah, I agree," I heard my mother say as I eavesdropped from the hallway. "I think he should become a lawyer, because God knows we need more of those fuckers."

She hung up the phone and called out, "Get out here, Shawn. I know you're behind that door. I can hear you breathing."

I walked from around the corner. Mom stared at me.

"That counselor, Mister..." she paused. "Mister whatever-the-hell... he said you were deluded in your goal to be a pro wrestler."

I had no comment.

"Do you think you're deluded?" she asked.

It seemed an unfair question to ask a seventeen year old. Years ago the man rumored to be my father, who I'd seen on a total of three occasions during my lifetime, had informed me there wasn't a snowball's chance in hell he was my real father and that this fact was one of the few things in his life he was honestly proud of. Why he hated me so much I couldn't fathom, being that I'd barely ever spoken to him. But then, he seemed to hate the world, and chances are I was simply lumped in with the package.

All I knew was professional wrestlers were big, muscular, unafraid, and seemingly confident in themselves. Was I deluded? Quite possibly. But at seventeen years old, I had no idea, nor did I care. All I knew was that these men were what I aspired to be.

"I don't know," I told my mom.

She kneeled down before me. "Don't let any of these people tell you what you can be," she said quietly. "Dream your own dream."

Crazy as she was, my mother was the only person who seemed to understand me and my desire to be a pro wrestler, to be larger than life. Larger than who I actually was. Maybe it was the only way I felt I could match my mom's image, because she certainly lived without seeming care. Capable of amazing rage and tenderness, she confessed to me one time when I was around eleven she'd actually robbed a bank in one of the neighborhoods a few hours from where we lived. Walked in wearing a baseball cap and wig, handed them a note, and walked out with close to two thousand dollars in cash. She donated it to the local animal rescue center.

The crime went unsolved.

By the spring before I was set to graduate high school Mom had gone off lithium completely. As the days grew longer she seemed to grow more and more agitated. Perhaps she was impatient. Her rages, tantrums, and threats of suicide became commonplace enough for me to simply reply, "Yes dear," whenever she bellowed them.

Then came the night I'd always been preparing for but wasn't quite ready to handle. It was a Tuesday in June, just a few weeks after my high school graduation, when I got a phone call from someone who identified herself as Officer Harlow. She told me there had been a bad accident and could I get over to the hospital right away.

Maybe it was the somber tone of the woman's voice, or a certain eruption within me that was spewing a mixture of dread and relief, as though a spiritual umbilical cord had just been snapped. "She's dead, isn't she?" I asked.

"I'm very sorry," was the reply.

I told myself I wasn't.

The death was ruled accidental, which was generous to say the least. How anyone could have driven down a road near where they lived that had a twenty mile an hour speed limit and plowed into a dead end ravine with enough velocity to send them flying through the windshield "accidentally" was beyond me. When I identified her, Mom's face was a map of haphazard gashes and dangling flesh. One of her eyes looked ready to fall out. It seemed impossible that this wrecked casing could ever have housed such an uncontrollable and insatiable mind.

I knew this had been no accident. This had been my mother carrying out her life's dream. She'd finally escaped herself.

At her funeral, I was painfully aware that all eyes were on me. Aunts, Uncles,

Cousins, good people all. No doubt they were wondering what the heck to say to this eighteen year-old kid who'd just lost his bipolar mother to an obvious suicide. Even more disturbing were the unspoken thoughts: would I turn out to be like her? I would later learn that guilt by association streaks through families of all kinds: alcoholics, homosexuals, overachievers. Nobody's immune.

I felt a hand on my shoulder. It was my Uncle Ted, a tall rugged man whose beard always reminded me of Sterling Hayden. "Just because your mom had problems," he murmured to me. "That doesn't mean there's anything wrong with you."

I would've liked to believe him, but I had my doubts. Hadn't I spent my teenaged afternoons not throwing a ball around like any red-blooded American boy, but jumping around battling fantastical villains on a stolen high jump mat? Not to mention that my guidance counselor had called me "deluded," and the woman who'd given birth to me had just committed suicide.

The family gathered around. "Anything you want, Shawn." Aunt Brenda assured me. "Any help you need. We'll be there for you."

I took a deep breath. "I want to go to Los Angeles and train to be a professional wrestler."

Aunt Brenda coughed. Uncle Ted looked around worriedly. Uncle Terry offered up a nervous laugh.

"My train leaves tomorrow," I told them. Then I busted out a biceps pose, linking my one arm with the other.

Here I was, striking a pose in front of the coffin where my mother's body lay. To my family's credit, all they did was nod and wish me well and guarantee me their full support.

We were staying in a hotel about three blocks from the funeral home. Later that night, I left my room and made my way down to the bar with the intent to have a few cocktails and fortify myself for the fact that I was hopping on a train the next day that would rattle toward parts unknown. I'd just stepped past the artificial plants that lined the entrance to the bar when I heard my Uncle Ted's voice: "He seems to be holding up well. I watched him during the ceremony. He didn't cry at all."

His tone sounded proud. I stopped and pressed myself against the wall, hoping to hear more praise.

The next verdict belonged to my Aunt Muriel. "Pro wrestling? That's crazy."

"I'm happy as long as he doesn't jump off a fucking bridge." This from Uncle Terry.

"But pro wrestling?" Muriel questioned. "*Why?*"

I went back up to my room, wondering the same thing.

The train to Los Angeles took three days. On the way, a woman sat on the seat next to me with such authority I didn't think to point out that there were plenty of empty seats surrounding us. She was smiling so widely I assumed she was either a prostitute or a serial killer. She turned out to be a Born Again Christian. She introduced herself as Dalila. Her very pleasant face sat atop a body that was, in her words, "thickened with age and past sin." She had a way of making sure her enormous breasts would smack into my arm as she testified to me about how her church had saved her.

"If you'd caught me before I'd been saved," she told me more than once. "You and I would probably be sinning as we speak."

I nodded, smiled, and took a sip from the flask I thanked the Good Lord I'd thought to bring along for the trip.

As the miles rolled on Dalila told me about how she, being one of God's soldiers, saw it her duty to enlighten others about God's word. "I want to save the world," she cooed, her left breast colliding with my elbow.

I sipped from my flask. "How?" I asked.

"All you've got to do is ask God and be saved," she answered with a smile.

We were passing through Colorado on the second day when, after a pleasant afternoon of many sips from my flask, I wondered out loud if my mom was in Heaven.

"Oh my God," Dalila gasped. "Your mother is dead? I'm so sorry."

"Thanks," I said. "Yeah, she killed herself last Tuesday."

Dalila's sympathetic frown furrowed itself into one of distaste. "She killed herself? That's a sin! That's against the word of God."

"God was watching as she did it," I suggested. "Why didn't He do anything to stop it?"

Dalila was busy shaking her head. "I'm sorry, Shawn. But your mother is burning in hell."

This shocked me. Certainly, Jane Michals had been no angel. She'd verbally abused me pretty much all my life, and had often mistaken me for a catcher's mitt. Still, I didn't think these were grounds for dismissal to eternal damnation. Maybe a nice purgatory, where she could sit and think about what she'd done. Or think about whatever the hell she wanted to, as long as she wasn't within throwing distance of me.

But here this stranger was condemning my mom to an eternity of fire and brimstone.

I laughed out loud at Dalila as I realized she would make a great pro wrestler. She had her gimmick down pat. One of God's soldiers, the ultimate babyface. She'd been the ultimate heel back in her "days of debauchery" but had now seen the light. However, she went into no detail about either episode. She offered no concrete evidence of her past sins, and also there wasn't any specific proof that she was now "saved." All she had was her words, which she claimed to be the words of God.

"Dalila," I told her, my own words unwinding from who knew where. "If you let me take you into the bathroom and have wild debauched sex with me, I will be saved." My voice, a bit slurred at this stage, grew louder. "I will see the Lord's light, and I will become a servant of the almighty! But shall ye not submit to my request, you will be responsible for sending me upon the road to sin! And I will henceforth be a villain, a servant of dark forces eager to bring about the demise of your so called Lord and master!"

By now I had risen to my feet, and people were staring at me. I was hooked on the attention. This is what I craved.

"The truth is that my mother was not responsible for her own death. I was. I am the one you want cast down to the gates of hell!" I intoned, liking the sound of this. Not only did it let my mom off the hook for suicide, it allowed me to assume the identity of unthinkable evil. I'd certainly wished her dead often enough. Who's to say she wasn't just following my mental commands?

Dalila quickly scurried out of her seat and into the aisle. I shouted after her: "Will you join me, my reformed one, in vanquishing the foolishness of tears for those who have come before, and embrace a path of damning victory!"

Though I had no idea what the hell I was saying at this point, Dalila may have, because she was rushing off down the aisle as if Satan himself were in hot pursuit. "I'll pray for you!" she called back.

The train car's other passengers slowly looked away from me. I thought I saw one of them, an older woman, wink in my direction, but this may have been simply a vodka-fueled hallucination. Regardless, I sat down quite satisfied. I'd defended my dead mother, chased away a soldier of God, and cut my first pro wrestling promo.

I was ready for anything Los Angeles or the world of professional wrestling could throw at me. So I thought.

❧   ❧   ❧

Wally Sanderson's Pro Wrestling Academy was in a rundown part of East L.A. Its green walls were peeling with old paint and still had slogans such as "KIM SUX BALLS" and "PETER TAKES IT UP THE ASS;" evidence of the space's former life as a classroom for juveniles who were wards of the state.

Now a wrestling ring lay in the middle of the floor, and the place smelled of beer, stale sweat, and baby oil. The beer came from the can constantly present in Wally's hand; the sweat and baby oil belonged to me and the other students, results of our workouts and the gooey substance we were constantly having to smear on ourselves at Wally's insistence.

"Get used to it, boys!" Wally would bellow. The man never spoke in anything resembling a quiet tone. "In the IWO, they swear by this stuff! It makes you shine under the lights!"

The IWO was the International Wrestling Organization. For up and coming wrestlers, it was the Promised Land. They had the biggest names in wrestling, annual events like SlamMania, SummerBash, and a host of other Pay-Per-View events where, before a worldwide audience of millions, superhumans did battle with one another.

Even though the outcomes of these clashes were predetermined, Wally made it clear to us this did not diminish the effort needed to conduct them. "Pro wrestling is not, as most people phrase it, 'fake.'" He told us on the first day of training. "It's a 'work.' There's a difference. If it were fake, wrestlers wouldn't need painkillers, steroids, and all the other shit they take just to get through their three hundred day a year travel schedule. They wouldn't suffer innumerable concussions and broken bones. Make no mistake, gentlemen. Professional wrestling is as real a sport and as real an art as they come."

For me the stage of pro wrestling offered the wonderful quality of an enigma, being that it was a world where no outsiders truly knew just exactly what was based in reality. As a writer is free to make up characters, those admitted to the fraternity of professional wrestling as performers are free to embrace any gimmick and transform themselves into whoever they want to be.

I knew who I wanted to be. I wanted to be the character I'd created on the train. In interviews, I boasted about slaughtering those who'd gotten in my way. I spoke of nothing meaning anything to me, caring about no one and strongly hinted that I'd committed matricide. "See you in hell, bitch," was my tag line I used after every interview. Though speaking to my upcoming opponent, I also held open the possibility I was speaking to my deceased mother.

In the ring I used foreign objects, raked eyes, choked people out past the referee's count of five, and oftentimes stared down at the canvas as though listening to orders from hell.

Wally loved my gimmick and encouraged me to "go deeper." Soon we were sharing beers after classes and he was asking me about my past.

"Do your parents know you're training?" he asked, the hint of mischief in his voice making becoming a professional wrestler on par with becoming an assassin.

I took my time answering. First I ordered a shot of tequila with a beer back. When they arrived I picked up the shot glass, I admit, for effect. "My parents are dead," I drawled, then slammed the shot and slapped the glass back on the bar. I took a hefty swallow of beer and stared in the mirror behind the bar as Wally gaped at me.

"That really true?" he asked. Though he could still be easily heard above the jukebox, it was the softest I'd heard him speak since I'd started training a month ago. "I kinda thought it might just be part of your gimmick and all."

"I I.D.'d my mother's body when her face looked like raw hamburger and didn't shed a tear. Hell," I added, "It was all I could do not to laugh."

I wasn't sure whether my last comment had been for effect or not.

"Damn, brother!" Wally hooted. "You *do* live the gimmick, don't you? Someone once wrote a book about that. Probably good advice, if you've got shit for brains."

I smiled back at my reflection. "That I've got," I said.

My family became a bit concerned when I told them about my training. They didn't mind that I was getting slammed on my back up to two hundred times a day on a plywood board, or getting chairs smacked over the top of my head. It was that I was doing all this without health insurance that worried them.

"You should really look into that," my dear Aunt Carrie advised me.

"Get some damn health insurance, Shawn!" Uncle Terry scolded me.

"Find a good Jewish girl and get married." This was from my Uncle Bert, who'd been at my mom's funeral weeping when I'd entered, and had promptly embraced and hugged me and voiced his sorrow for my loss while all the time, having never seen him before in my life, I was wondering who the hell he was.

I had no time to think about marriage, being that my pro wrestling career was in the process of taking off. Just four months after coming to Southern California I was wrestling in matches across the state. Not only that, but I was "going over," which in the pro wrestling world means winning. Promoters loved my irreverence, although there was a prickly incident at a Y.M.C.A. when, after a female voice kept yelling at me to "stick it where the sun doesn't shine," I leapt up on the turnbuckle, rotated my hips, and then grabbed my crotch while glaring at my agitator for the first time and telling her to "ride it where the sun don't shine, baby." To my chagrin I found myself addressing a girl who couldn't have been more than twelve years old.

But awkward encounters like this are all part of the pro wrestling world. On the whole promoters were pleased with me. I drew heat and drew money. With my gimmicked name, "The Weapon of Mass Destruction," I made a slow but steady climb to main event status in the world of independent wrestling throughout Southern California.

The climb was less than glamorous. There were nights spent in hotel rooms with me and two fellow wrestlers in the bed and three more sleeping on the floor. At restaurants one of us would buy the "all you can eat buffet" and then we'd all take turns using the plate. If the managers or servers caught on, our combined weight usually prevented them from saying anything. We called this the "six for one" special.

Our principal mode of transport was a van with six or seven of us crammed inside. Most of us enjoyed our drinks, and were constantly having to go to the bathroom. This led to frantic instances when we'd have to urinate in empty bottles then cap them hurriedly. If the driver was a scoundrel (and being a pro wrestler, it was a given he was), he'd make sure to weave a bit while one of us was trying to navigate our aim. So my early wrestling career, in addition to getting pounded on every night, also consisted of traveling hundreds of miles in a van smelling of sweaty wrestling garb, beer, and urine.

There was also the business of payoffs. One of the more memorable incidents occurred with a promoter in Burbank. He claimed to have spent the $2500 he'd promised all of the wrestlers on some kind of insurance bond the venue had demanded at the last minute.

The promoter, despite being maybe 120 pounds sopping wet, went by the moniker of Mr. Mongo. "I've got nothing for you," he told us, after the show was over and all fifty-six paying fans had filed out of the high school gymnasium.

We wrestlers began to mill in menacingly. It was only a matter of seconds before one of us pulverized this lying asshole.

To my surprise minutes passed and no one did anything but snarl, grimace, and make vague threats about "going downtown on Mongo's ass." Here we were, all at least two hundred pounds apiece, with names like "The Demon" Daniel Livings and Ricky "You're my Bitch" Rich, and we'd just finished displaying our dominance over one another in front of dozens of fans. Still we were hesitant to take actual physical action against a guy who was built like a stork, even though he was steadfastly refusing to pay us money we'd earned. Our inability to act made him grow more arrogant as he seemed to realize we weren't in a wrestling ring and outside of a wrestling ring most of us weren't bloodthirsty animals who wanted only to hurt others.

Then suddenly a large woman pushed through us and told Mr. Mongo that we deserved to be paid. She was the mother of Bobby Blitzer, who worked a football player gimmick.

"You better give these boys their money!" she shouted at Mr. Mongo.

He sneered at her. "Just back off, you fat bitch—"

Now Bobby Blitzer was a pretty mellow soul outside the ring. But at these words, all two hundred and forty pounds of him leapt over a table and grabbed Mongo by the collar. "You don't ever talk to my mother that way, you little prick!" he yelled.

Mr. Mongo immediately emptied his pockets, scattering money across the floor ranging in denominations from ten dollars to a nickel.

We wrestlers descended upon the bounty like a pack of wolves. In the interest of brotherhood, we all took roughly the same amount. Our average pay for that night was eight bucks, and we had Bobby's mom to thank for it.

I caught myself wondering if my mom would have done the same. Probably not. She would've just hurled a fire extinguisher at Mr. Mongo's head, then picked up other random projectiles to whip at us for not having the guts to kick the crap out of him in the first place.

Crazy woman, I told myself, while watching Bobby and his mom share a hug.

❧   ❧   ❧

"When I say pick me up, you scrawny little shit, I mean *pick me up!*"

These were the first words I ever heard my idol, Tank Gohan, say in person. It was backstage at the San Bernardino Arena. Tank was addressing his son, whose ring name was Gunner Gohan. Gunner (whose real name was in fact Gunner) stood about 5'9" to his father's 6'5" and appeared to weigh at least a hundred pounds less.

It was just nine months into my dream career, and that night I was set to take on my friend, Beautiful Jake Steed, in an "extreme match" that we'd been planning for a month. Bottles, chains, frying pans - all were going to be used as weapons. We'd even scavenged an old rusted kitchen sink from a junkyard in South Central L.A. It was to be my first night "juicing," or bleeding in the ring. Tank, meanwhile, was in the main event, in which he would wrestle his son.

Though as far as venues went the 800 seat San Bernardino Arena was a step up for me, it was quite a few steps down for Tank, being that he'd main-evented for several years in the IWO, enjoying a brief run as World Champion. He would boast in interviews about "manning his cannons" and "hanging and banging with his guns armed to the teeth," along with various other militaristic threats directed at his foes in the ring.

Now I was a bit shocked and awed to see Tank in the flesh, promising in what sounded like a much more real voice to legitimately beat the living crap out of his son if he proved unable to body slam him in their upcoming match. "You can do it, kid," Tank said. "'Cause if you don't, you know what I can do in that ring. You might get hurt."

"Yeah, Pop, I know." Gunner's reply was a mumble.

Truth be told, I didn't want to look too closely at Tank or his son. Part of the reason was because I'd always harbored a jealously of kids like Gunner. Growing up, I'd always imagined what a wonderful dad Tank would make. Now here he was making threats to his son just because the kid wasn't as genetically gifted as he was. True, the creature I'd once thought of as my dad had long ago told me he hated my guts and wanted nothing to do with me, but at least this declaration had been made over the phone and was devoid of promised physical violence.

There was plenty of physical violence in my match with my buddy Jake. Fortunately I was prepared for it, being that from the time we'd started changing for our match to the time we made our ring entrances we'd polished off a liter of vodka. "Thins the blood," Jake had assured me. "Makes us juice easier."

He needn't have worried. As we bashed each other over the head with assorted household items (including the kitchen sink), my forehead opened up and I was gushing blood everywhere. It was when Jake chucked a pan at my head that I remembered in what seemed like forever the first time my mom had thrown something at me. It had been an alarm clock. It had cut open my forehead and I'd been in shock when I'd seen the sight of my own blood. Five or six years old maybe, I'd gone into the kitchen while she continued screaming. I'd grabbed a knife and cut at my forehead again and again until she stopped screaming and started crying.

That was the first time I'd felt any kind of power over anyone in my life.

In the midst of my match with Jake, I got the same feeling. The more Jake and I cut ourselves open with blades hidden in our finger tape, the more fans chanted "Holy shit" and "This is awesome!" It wasn't until we reached the planned finish of the match, which involved me leaping off a ladder and driving Jake through a table lined with fluorescent light bulbs (chosen because of their easy propensity to shatter) that I realized I felt a bit lightheaded from the loss of so much blood.

A pro wrestling match can sometimes be described as a lovemaking session. No matter how tired you are, you try and give your partner some kind of a finish. So I began to climb the ladder, which suddenly seemed taller than I'd expected, and as

I passed the rung that bore an explicit warning not to stand above it I wondered how in the hell I was going to explain this to a therapist in my middle-aged years.

After a few rickety seconds of balancing precariously on the top step, I threw myself off in a half leap and half fall and landed on top of a prone Jake Steed. The light bulbs burst in an explosion of tiny shards and the table broke in two, just like it was supposed to. I collapsed on top of Jake and heard a one-two-three! My right hand was raised in victory, and I used my left to sweep blood from my eyes. My vision was blurry but I was able to make out people on their feet applauding me, chanting the name "Weapon."

Bleeding profusely, my body aching and burnt, I felt no pain whatsoever. So much adrenaline was running through me, I didn't feel a damn thing.

Backstage, there was an onsite physician and he stitched my forehead up as I weaved in and out of coherency.

"Thirty at the most," he said, when he was done.

"Thirty stitches?" I asked, unable to mask a bit of pride.

"No, fourteen stitches. I was predicting how old you're gonna live to be if you don't get out of this business."

I was too spent to ask him whether he was kidding or not.

Later on, as I changed into my street clothes in the locker room I heard a voice. "Tough stuff out there, brother."

Though I'd downed a couple sips of post-match vodka along with four Vicodin, I wasn't so out of it I didn't recognize that growl which had held me glued to the television every Saturday morning. I looked up from where I was struggling to navigate my foot into one of my cowboy boots and saw Tank Gohan in the doorway.

His arms were still remarkably large, and though his hairline had begun to recede his face had managed to retain a youthful vigor that made him look, as my mom had once put it, "like a mustached teddy bear." The only thing that seemed a bit off was his skin, which boasted an oddly exaggerated orange, the way produce can display inflated colors under grocery store lights.

"Thanks, Tank." I said shyly. "Was your son… was he able to get you up all right?"

Tank grunted. "Sure," he said. "Anyway, just wanted to say you looked good out there."

As he turned to go, I yelped, "Tank!"

He paused, and when he looked back the amused curiosity in his expression embarrassed me. I must've sounded desperate, like a dog barking after its master.

"You ever been hurt?" I asked him. This man, who in the ring had made a career of kicking out of his opponents' most devastating "finishing maneuvers" and coming back with a flurry of faked punches and a knee drop off the top rope to win his match, stared at me for a long time. I knew that his wife had recently filed for divorce and his daughter was shooting a reality show about how horrible it was to be his daughter.

"Everything hurts you, kid. Even when it's a work. Life… life is…" Tank paused, lost at the kernel of his wisdom. In interviews on T.V. he'd always seemed so confident of his next word, rolling past conclusions as easily as an armored tank over grass.

Here he was now taking on reality, a confounding enemy. Still, I hung on his words.

"It hurts," he concluded. "You can cry about it like a wuss, or you can keep lacing up your boots."

"Keep manning your cannons," I recited, before I could stop myself.

A smile slowly made its way onto his face, brushing up the edges of his mustache. "Keep manning your cannons, brother," he said.

Then he was gone.

Later that night I lay in bed thinking about what Tank had said. I pondered my life and what had brought me to this point; getting paid a hundred bucks to do to my forehead what supposedly troubled people did to themselves. *Cutting, Self-inflicted harm, Third-Party Related Abuse...* the doctors had names for it, as they seem to have names for everything. I'd read somewhere that it was supposed to be a coping mechanism of some sort.

Thinking made my brow cringe and strain the stitches that were keeping my self-inflicted third-party related cut closed.

Weeks later, when the stitches dissolved, the wound was still tender. It hurts, I reminded myself. Damned if I was gonna fucking cry about it.

❀ ❀ ❀

A year into my wrestling career, the International Wrestling Organization came to town for television tapings. Wally called me and told me they needed a few "jobbers," which were better defined as "guys who will lose in three minutes to superstars." But, Wally made sure to point out, we would be getting paid two hundred dollars for three minutes work.

"Plus, you can make an impression!" Wally assured us. "The big boys are always watching for youngsters ready to rise to the next level. And being that I like to think of you all as my trainees, I don't think I need to remind you all that it's customary for a performer, be they an actor, a gymnast, or a musician, to kick up ten percent of your pay to your agent."

So basically we were getting a hundred and eighty bucks to pretend to get our asses kicked in three minutes.

I was paired up with a fellow local Southern California wrestler, Gary Lockes. He was a beefy guy who was in training to become a professional poker player. Luckily for him, his fiancé was not only beautiful but also heir to a ketchup fortune. Gary claimed he "dabbled" in pro wrestling because he "loved to mix it up," but was always extremely protective of his face. Privately he'd confessed to me that it turned his fiancé on to see him wrestling other men wearing tights.

That night, there were ten thousand people in the arena. As we walked out through the curtain, I was stunned at how small the crowd looked when compared to seeing it on television. Kind of like seeing a movie star in person; they're usually smaller than you'd imagine.

Still, there were thousands and thousands of people, and given that I was used to wrestling in front of dozens and dozens of people, maybe hundreds and hundreds on a good night, I was pretty psyched. As an added bonus, though as wrestlers we were about as equal in status to extras who are slaughtered in a nameless heap in a war movie, the fans lining ringside still reached out to touch us as we walked past.

I became enamored of the attention and slowed down to touch the outstretched hands of so many people that the referee had to shout at me to get the hell in the ring before *he* jumped out and pinned my ass in three minutes.

Gary and I were wrestling a pair of Samoans called The Headdrinkers. Fatoo and Shamoo. Each stood well over six feet, weighed at least three hundred pounds, and looked as though they ate bottle caps for breakfast and returned for the bottle at lunchtime. Given their imposing presence, none of the other IWO wrestlers ever mined the potential humor the gimmicked names of Fatoo and Shamoo offered. Staring across the ring at them, even though I knew this was a "work" and would last no more than three minutes, I was scared as hell.

At first, the match seemed to go well. When their manager frightened me with a skull steaming with dried ice ("Sell it like it's death itself, brotha," he'd advised me backstage) I thought I did an admirable job of shrieking like a banshee and running to my corner. But after I tagged in Gary, he made the mistake of falling back about three feet before Fatoo hit him with a dropkick, prompting a chant of "bullshit" and "take two" from the ringsiders. Shamoo then threw Gary out of the ring and slammed him face first on the metal steps in the corner of the ring apron. When Gary was thrown back into the ring, I saw he was busted open the hard way, meaning he hadn't cut himself on purpose. The corner of the steps had caught the space between his upper lip and his nose, and the blood running down had already formed a crimson goatee.

Before I knew what was happening Gary had tagged me in and I was in the hands of two very pissed off 300 plus pound Samoans who took me into the ropes. One of them, I forget whether it was Fatoo or Shamoo, whispered to me. "Backdrop. And you'd better *fly,* asshole."

The last time I'd heard someone order me to jump so emphatically had been when my mom had shouted at me to leap off our house. I'd been able to back out of her challenge, but then of course my mother hadn't been capable of physically snapping me in two. This time I had no choice; I'd always wanted to be a pro wrestler. Now I was one. Buy the ticket, take the ride.

I hit the ropes and ran back in the direction of two massive men who were crouched, ready to launch me into the air. I could hear Mom singing softly, *Merrily Merrily Merrily Merrily, Life is But a Dream*. Well, if I was going to die I was going to die like my insane mother. Full speed. When I placed my hands on the backs of my opponents and felt them push up, I jumped with all my strength. Between their thrust and mine I must've clocked a good three seconds airtime, which is a long time if you're doing a somersault fifteen feet above the ground.

I landed fine, tucking my neck and landing on the top of my back just like I'd been taught. I heard the crowd "oooh" and "ahhh." I opened my eyes and when I saw the arena lights glaring down at me I assumed I was still alive. I rolled over and there were the men who'd launched me into orbit staring at me, mouths open in shock. One of them quickly went to pick me up. "Jesus, kid," he whispered. "Are you okay?"

"Fine," I whispered back. And with all the adrenaline rushing through me, I believed I was. It had just been another bump. No big deal.

The match finished with me getting pinned and Gary getting an impromptu chair slammed into his face as he came in the ring to "protect" me after the pinfall.

I was helped by the referee along the path to the backstage area. The same fans who'd wanted to touch me just minutes ago now jeered and laughed and shouted out instructions to the nearest fast food restaurants that were hiring.

Backstage I went through the curtain and immediately started walking normally. To my amazement a lot of the featured IWO stars were assembled, and they gave me affirming nods and complimented me on my willingness to put my opponents over.

Victor Thomas, the owner of the International Wrestling Organization himself, approached me with an outstretched hand and a bemused smile. At 6'4" and easily two hundred and fifty pounds, his physique was a blatant slap in the face to Congressmen who spent more time worrying about athletes taking steroids than the fact that the country's Social Security Fund was going to be bankrupt in twenty years.

"Tell me," Victor said in a voice that seeped authority. "Can you take bumps like that all the time?"

How in the hell did I know? I'd been running from a ghost in that ring, bumping for my life.

"Absolutely," I assured the big man.

"Good," he said, nodding. "That's good."

Later that night, one of the agents, a former pro wrestler who'd had a drill sergeant gimmick, came ambling up to me. "Hey, kid," he barked, holding out a business card. "Give a call to our office back east tomorrow. We may have a place for you."

When I woke up that night, sandwiched between two of my fellow jobbers in our sixty dollar a night motel room, it didn't matter to me that that my back was throbbing and my neck felt as though it were about to fall off my shoulders and roll under the bed, taking my head with it.

The IWO had a place for me. I got out of bed as gingerly as possible so as not to awaken my bedmates. Then I stared in the hotel room mirror and flexed. The reflection staring back at me was a 'roided up, tanned "Weapon of Mass Destruction." A character of my own design.

I caught myself humming *Merrily Merrily Merrily Merrily, Life is but—*

I stopped myself. Life was real. I was real. The head of the largest professional wrestling organization in the world had confirmed my existence.

My mom had followed her road. Now I would follow mine.

The road I followed for the next month involved me getting into the ring and getting the crap knocked out of me every night. My name said it all: I was introduced simply as FitzMichael. The name was Victor Thomas's idea; according to him it was the quintessential name for "a young man from the provinces."

Even though steroids and gym sessions had bulked me up to 210 pounds, my height of 5'10" kept me at a decided physical disadvantage when compared with some of the monsters in the IWO. One in particular was Jesse Lee Hamhock. He was a big grizzled Texan and was currently enjoying a run as the International Wrestling Organization Heavyweight Champion. He liked to drink, shoot out street signs with his shotgun, and haze younger wrestlers.

I was advised by everyone in the locker room to try and get on his good side as quickly as possible, but I made a misstep early on when one night I declared *The Dukes of Hazzard* one of the campiest television series in history.

"Say what now?" Jesse asked, turning in his chair real slow.

We were in a bar, after a house show in Kansas City. Or it may have been Des Moines or Topeka or the damn moon for all I knew. After a few weeks life on the road had already become a blur of gyms, airports, arenas and bars.

This particular bar had deer heads on the wall and rebel flags draped above both the men and ladies bathrooms, so looking back it probably wasn't the best of places to mock a show that celebrated characters with names such as Uncle Jesse, Daisy, and Enos. Still, all gathered at our table, Sammy "Hit-Man" Hardway, Tommy Agro, Davey "Five-Finger" Jammer... they seemed to appreciate my impersonation of Boss Hogg and Sheriff Roscoe P. Coltrane as being latent homosexual lovers. Everyone was laughing like hell. Everyone, that is, except Jesse Lee Hamhock, who was seething unmistakably in my direction. The veins in his neck were as tight as violin strings but about a hundred times thicker.

"Funny kid," was all he said. Then he went back to drinking his beer.

A week later, I was wrestling a non-title match against Hamhock (I was way too new and far down on the ladder to be considered a legitimate contender) and he introduced me to his "patented finishing maneuver," the Forearm From Down South. After he slammed his beefy forearm across my throat my body did a great imitation of a slam dunked basketball as I dropped to the mat, followed by a great imitation of a bouncing basketball as the back of my head ricocheted off the canvas.

"How funny was that, kid?" he snarled at me before performing an imitation of Roscoe's laugh that I would've maybe even laughed at had it not felt as if my larynx had just been crushed.

The situation grew progressively weirder. Nights after shows, Jesse took to stalking me in the locker room showers. "You need a lathering, funny kid?" he'd ask with a sneer so serious it was frightening to think there might actually be a reasonable response I could come up with. Dressed in just his trunks, cowboy boots and hat, he'd make grabbing motions at my naked body as I leapt around running water trying to avoid him.

When I tried to subtly bring up that any reasonable court of law might consider this harassment, my fellow wrestlers simply shrugged.

"All in the game," Too Cool Taylor assured me.

"He'll get over it eventually," Studly Steve Simpson shrugged.

"Don't ever slip in the shower," Chainsaw Charlie Higgins advised. "He sees it as a sign of weakness."

I stopped showering at the arenas. At nights I'd sit in my hotel room and wonder what the hell I'd gotten myself into. I wished over and over I could go back to my "Weapon of Mass Destruction" character. That creation had never known fear,

or pain, or loss. He'd never felt anything. He'd had hell on his side.

Then a few nights later, hell did
indeed break loose.

It occurred, once again, at a bar after
a show.

I was having a few cocktails with Jammer and Agro, two guys who were, like me,
pretty new to the IWO and all its eccentricities.

"Hey, funny kid!" Jesse roared from
across the bar.

As a rule, pro wrestlers and bars are a
combustible combination. Add up liquor,
heightened testosterone levels from the
steroids we were supposedly being tested
for, the social pecking order that seems
to permeate any business, and you've
got…

Well, in this case I had a 310 pound
Texan coming at me with a beer in both
hands and a phony smile on his face.

"Hey, funny kid," he said, "How's this
taste?"

Jesse then performed an exaggerated
fall and in the process smothered my face
with one of the beers.

I licked my lips. Actually, the beer
tasted pretty good. By this point I'd had
several drinks and was well along the
way enough to accept this as a backward
attempt at a peace offering.

"Could use a vodka shooter," I commented. Wittily, I thought.

Apparently, Jesse found my wit somewhat lacking. He scowled at me. "Bet it tasted better than your mama's pussy does," he spat.

Nobody else seemed to think this comment was out of the ordinary. Then again nobody knew about my mom killing herself. Nobody really knew me, least of all this asshole, grin on his face after he'd just spit on my mother's memory.

I charged, catching him on his left knee. He went down on top of me and began to hammer away at my head. These blows were no harder than the ones he'd used on me in the ring, and therefore I was used to them. But what Jesse wasn't used to was my right fist cracking the hell out of his jaw, and then my foot slamming into his left knee.

Jesse howled in pain as I rose. A few of our fellow wrestlers tried to push me back but I shoved them away.

"My mother's dead, you goddamn piece of shit!" I screamed at Jesse Hamhock, IWO Heavyweight Champion, as he lay writhing at my feet. "And you know what? I killed her! I'm the only one allowed to say anything about that filthy stinking no good psycho bitch!"

Hearing myself say these words shocked me. I couldn't have really hated her that

much, could I? She had, after all, given
me life. And she'd certainly been interesting enough to grow up with.

"She wasn't a bitch, per se," I specu-
lated, half to myself and half to the now
silent bar. "She was…"

Insane? Unique? Terrifying, because
I thought desperately that by becoming
someone else I could escape her shadow
that promised me, as her sole offspring,
a tortured life ending in suicide?

I turned and left the bar, the question unanswered.

To my shock, I wasn't fired after this
incident. On the contrary I began to move
up the card, wrestling semi-main events
and actually being allowed to win matches.

The boys now treated me with respect,
if not outright trepidation. When I suggested various spots we could do in a
match, they readily agreed. In the locker
room, Jesse and I kept our distance from
one another. I admit I observed his limp
with a bit of satisfaction.

Victor Thomas seemed to be watching
me a bit more than he had in the past.
Whether that was good or bad I couldn't
determine. But about a month after what
had been deemed by the boys as "the night
the lights went out in FitzMichael,"
(very few of them knew my real name), we
were at a TV taping when Victor called

me over to where he was standing beside a catering table.

"You're working with Jesse tomorrow night," he said.

I nodded. "Okay."

"And you're going over."

I nodded again, this time a bit more warily. "Okay."

"You know what that means, right?"

I nodded again, waiting for the punch line. And it came.

"You're going to become the new International Wrestling Organization Heavyweight champion," he told me.

He may as well have suggested I was in line to become the next Pope. I laughed. "I can't be the champion." I corrected my boss. "I'm… I was a jobber six months ago."

Victor's face contracted a bit, then expanded, as it always did whenever anyone was stupid enough to contradict him. "First off," he said. "I run this organization. If *I* say you can be the champion, you can goddamn well be the champion. You've got what Tank Gohan had. Momentum. It's all over the Internet, all those promos you did in that two-bit Southern California promotion where you said you killed your mother. Where you said you looked over her grave and saw her going down to hell."

I swallowed. I didn't know what was more frightening; that I had been half-drunk at the time I cut those promos, or that as they say, *en vino es veritas*. Wine and truth dancing hand in hand through the lily fields. "But I never exactly..." I began.

"Doesn't matter!" he cut me off. "They're the stuff of genius. Like that guy, the rapper who's named after a candy..."

"Eminem?" I proposed.

"Yeah! You're like him. He's made millions of dollars rapping about how much he hates his mother. All kids hate their parents. It's a great gimmick! And tomorrow night, in your hometown of Los Angeles..."

"My hometown's Chicago actually-"

"Not anymore," Victor snapped with the impatience of someone who isn't interrupted. Ever. "You, FitzMichael, were born in that arena in Los Angeles when you took that huge backdrop. That's what got you noticed. And tomorrow night in that same arena, you're going to win the World's Heavyweight Championship. Now how's that make you feel?"

Like I needed a fucking drink.

That night in my hotel room I found a drink in the minibar. I quickly exhausted the three vodkas in there so I moved onto the whiskey, and then the gin. I was alone. Victor had sworn me to secrecy regarding the title change. Nobody but Victor, Jesse, and myself were to know. I didn't want to take the chance of going down to the bar where all the other wrestlers were and accidentally telling them that I was about to achieve my dream tomorrow night and that I was completely terrified and didn't know why.

I was unscrewing the first mini bottle of rum when a knock came at the door. I weaved to my feet and answered it, thinking it was perhaps Room Service with a bottle of vodka I'd forgotten ordering.

There stood Jesse Lee Hamhock. Given the amount of alcohol I'd consumed I should have been able to screw up a bit of liquid courage, but all I could think was here at my door stood a walking refrigerator who wanted to do nothing more than pulverize me the night before I was supposed to pin him for a championship based on illusion.

"Mind if I come in and chew the cud?" he asked.

"Chew the...?" I stammered.

"Talk," he said. His voice was slow, maybe a bit drunk. Well, I thought, if he's gonna try and pound me it's gonna happen sooner or later. Might as well be sooner.

I opened the door and ushered him inside, my eyes darting this way and that in search of a potential weapon if need be.

"You gonna offer me a drink?" he asked.

I poured us both rum and cokes and dropped into a chair, making sure my back was to the wall.

"Just so's you know," he said. "Victor has been after me to lose the belt for a while now. Says my gimmick's done gone a little stale. I haven't really wanted to drop it. But I agreed to drop it to you."

"Why?" I asked. "Because I kicked your ass?"

Immediately I realized just how drunk I was. Only an intoxicated fool fried to the tonsils would brag to an extra-large Texan about kicking their ass.

Jesse only laughed.

"Naw, that wasn't it. But you got in some good shots. What sold me was what you said about your ma."

"I was drunk," I said.

"You're drunk now," he said. "She hurt you?"

I took a healthy swallow. "Yeah," I said quietly.

"Me too," he nodded. "My pa, I mean. He'd whip the living shit out of me and tell me it was for my own good."

Jesse stared into his drink. "Goddamnit, he was… some ways…" he said. "Some ways, he was a great man. Took care of Ma and me. But he was a bully. Liked to hurt people. So I just followed his example."

He sniffed once and slammed more of his drink. "Anyway, when you were honest about your mom, about how you really felt about her, I couldn't help but think about all the times I wanted to kill my old man. Never admitted it to myself, though."

"It's a tough thing to admit," I allowed.

"Reckon it is," he said. "That's why you were the one I chose to lose the belt to."

Jesse rose, and as I struggled to my feet his eyes roamed around the room and caught sight of the dozen or so miniature bottles of vodka, scotch, gin, etc.

"Damn, kid," he smiled. "That's another thing I like about you. You can put 'em away."

"I line 'em up," I admitted. "I knock 'em down."

The big man guffawed. "Shit, you oughta think about making that your catch phrase."

He ambled over to the door, but before he opened it he looked back at me. "What did your ma do to you to make you hate her so much?" he asked.

She'd threatened to kill me, told me she'd wished I'd never been born. But she'd also cared for me, taken me for my first ride on a bicycle, pointed at the stars in the sky and urged me to wish upon one. She'd told me that fear is the thief of dreams. She'd been as savage and brilliant as a hurricane.

"She left me," I whispered.

"Did you really kill her?"

Every fiber in me that made up the character I was desperate to be wanted to respond affirmatively. Of course I'd killed her; by killing her it would mean she hadn't killed herself, and that would mean she wasn't burning in hell. It would mean that in spite of how she'd treated me, I didn't really miss her.

"I…" I shrugged.

Jesse's massive head began to nod slowly.

"See 'ya tomorrow, champ," he said. The door closed softly behind him.

I lay back on the bed, thankful that the swirling ceiling made it impossible for me to concentrate on my thoughts.

I awoke to a melody. *Merrily, Merrily, Merrily, Merrily, life is but a dream…*

I bolted up in bed, suddenly too awake. The wall to my left was shadowed by tall thin stripes of dawn coming through the blinds. I got up and wandered over to the minibar, navigating best I could around the small empty bottles littering the floor like spent bullet cartridges. Thankfully there were two mini bottles left; one of rum and one of scotch. Hopefully enough to get Mom's stupid song out of my head.

I uncapped the rum and drank it down in three gulps, then stared into the mirror. My body was more impressive than it had any business being. A solid year of using steroids in greater quantity than any physician would legitimately prescribe had seen to that. My chest was so inflated I was able to flex my pectoral muscles as easily as I'd once been able to juggle two tennis balls when I'd been a kid. "A walking plate of armor," my mother had referred to me back in my Senior year of high school. "What the hell do you need that much protection from?"

I hadn't had the heart, or maybe the guts, to tell Mom the truth: from her, of course. But now, staring at the bulked up, shaven gladiator in the mirror, I wondered if there wasn't perhaps another deeper entity I was trying to shield this reflection from.

Myself?

Merrily Merrily Merrily Merrily, Mom sang. *Life is but a dream.*

If it's such a damned dream why did you want to wake up so bad?

"Where did you go?" I asked the mirror.

That afternoon, while I was in the locker room taping myself up for the match and taking a few swallows from a Vodka-rade (A combination of Gatorade, water and vodka mixed safely within the camou-flage of a Gatorade bottle in the inter-est of discretion), Jesse approached me. "Victor wants to see us," he said.

"Okay," I nodded.

As we walked side by side down the hallway toward Victor's dressing room, Jesse peered at me. "You been drinkin'?"

I shrugged.

His grin gave way to a laugh. "That's the idea. Only way to get to be a cham-pion is to be a first class fuck-up."

Jesse and I were still laughing when we entered Victor's dressing room. He smiled and gave us both a handshake before offering us a cup of coffee. Jesse took one. I declined.

"I think we should have a clean finish tonight." Victor told us.

"No problem with me," Jesse said.

I agreed.

We went over a finish and then Victor asked Jesse to please step outside so he could talk to me.

Jesse did so. Victor looked at me steadily. "You know," he said. "A lot of people, people who work for me, people I respect, have told me that putting the belt on you is a mistake."

I exhaled lightly, turning my head away so the smell of the vodka on my breath wouldn't be quite so aimed at my boss's face.

Victor sighed. "Don't make me look like a fool out there tonight, okay?"

I nodded. He put down two stapled bunches of paper in front of me. "These are scripts," he said. "Choose one. Memorize it. And deliver it tonight after you win the belt."

I reached out and put a hand on each of the thin scripts. "Which one do you want me to choose?" I asked.

This question seemed to please Victor. He sat back in his chair. "Why, whichever one ignites your passion," he drawled. "Now head on out and have a great match."

Back in the locker room, I looked over the two scripts. There was one in which I dedicated my title victory to my mother, who had, according to the script, "always served as an inspiration and guide before she was tragically taken from my life."

What a load of shit, I thought. It hadn't been tragic at all; it had been Jane Michals fulfilling her final goal.

I turned to the other script, which had me denouncing all people and stating that I had no allegiance to anyone, the fans included, and that I had even allowed my own mother to die because she threatened to impede my progress as a pro wrestling champion.

What a load of shit, I thought. She'd been the one who'd told me I could achieve whatever dream I wanted to.

"Shawn?" a voice came from my left.

I didn't respond. Months of being referred to by my gimmick name had made me immune to my real one.

"Fitzmichael?"

I snapped my head up. It was David Black, the referee that was going to work my match with Jesse for the title.

"Yeah?" I asked him.

"You and Jesse are up next. You ready?"

I brought the Vodkarade bottle to my lips and downed the last swallow. After I set it down, I looked at the two scripts in either hand, one proclaiming me a hero and one proclaiming me a demon. I slapped them both together.

"Ready as I'll ever be," I said.

For those of you who saw the match you know it wasn't exactly the greatest title match in IWO history. Truth is my mind was spinning from too many thoughts and just enough vodka to really remember much. I do remember that at one point as Jesse was lifting me up for a suplex he whispered to me, "Shit kid, you look like you're gonna puke."

I almost did puke, but managed to swallow it back. We took the match home with a spot that had me leap over Jesse and then roll him up into a small package. Three slaps of the mat later, I was the International Wrestling Organization Heavyweight Champion.

The applause surprised me. Chants of "FitzMichael" swelled as I was handed the championship belt.

It was the stuff of my dreams, with thousands of fans in an arena heaping approval on me while millions more watched on television. I'd come a long way from when I'd cut my first promo on a train in front of twenty frightened passengers.

There was another difference; back then I'd known what to say and who I wanted to be. Now, I had no idea. When the ring announcer handed me the microphone suddenly all the faces staring at me, a freshly crowned champion, became as intimidating as a firing squad.

"Ladies and gentlemen, I thank you." I said.

This went over well enough, eliciting a slight cheer from the crowd.

"I've always been uncertain about things," I went on. "I've always been uncertain about one person in particular. Bottom line is, I can't say whether I loved or hated her. I can't say whether I love or hate you. I can't say whether I love or hate myself."

Back in the days when professional wrestling was more a carnival act rather than a business traded on the New York Stock Exchange, there'd been a joke the wrestlers shared: *What has thirty-two teeth, an IQ of ninety, and a prison record?*

Answer: *The first five rows of any pro wrestling audience.*

But that night, as I bared my soul on national television about how lost I'd felt most of my life, and how following my passion to become a pro wrestler had been both a blessing and a curse, when I glanced over at the first couple rows in front of me on any side, I saw only silent contemplation. Perhaps these people came to shows in their roles of spectators for the same reason I desired to be a participant. Fans and heroes need one another, for without one the other can't exist, and in that mutual need is a desire for reassurance. Some might seek it from a sermon, some might seek it from a dropkick. But it's there, that need and that fulfillment, and such an unquenchable cycle is part of a greater puzzle, one of the many links that imbue life with such confounding potential for meaning.

My mom always seemed to not only understand this, but in her own way, cherish the challenge. She'd become so many different people, had so many different jobs and let identities fall from her as naturally as a snake sheds skins. She'd tested the heights of anger, of delight, and though she'd often apologized to me for what she'd done she'd never apologized to anyone for who she was, right up to that moment where she'd chosen to leave her body on her own terms. Though it hurt to love her, I couldn't deny that I still did.

I hadn't realized I'd been speaking out loud until I heard my voice crack as I uttered those last words.

I stopped speaking and saw eighteen thousand people around me cheering.

Then I felt the funniest thing. There were drops leaking out of me and crawling down my cheeks. My eyes actually hurt, it had been that long since I'd cried.

I held my belt aloft and climbed on top of a turnbuckle. I was alive, and life was but a dream. One day I would awaken, but for now I was content to keep dreaming, keep crying, keep living.

No matter how much it sometimes hurt.

LIFE IN THE PITZ

I graduated from a California State University with a degree in Radio, Television and Film, with an emphasis in Screenwriting. Which is sort of like having a degree in Picking One's Butt, with an emphasis in Finger Sniffing. I was fond of telling people the reason I'd gone to a State University was because I couldn't afford a fancy place like UCLA or USC. In truth, I probably could've gone to UCLA, had they not rejected me when I tried to get into their program. The essay I offered for submission compared Patrick Dempsey's 1980s high school comedy *Can't Buy Me Love,* in which a high school geek bribes the hottest girl in the Senior class to pretend to like him so that he may gain access to their clique, to the movie *Six Degrees of Separation,* in which Will Smith cons his way into Upper Class Manhattan society by pretending to be Sidney Poitier's son.

The topic seemed like a good idea at the time.

While Patrick Dempsey would go on to television stardom and Will Smith would become one of the biggest names in movies, I obtained my degree in Butt Picking and went off looking for work.

I had an opportunity to become an intern at one of the Big Three (at least at that time) entertainment agencies in L.A. However, my friends fervently warned me against this path. Not that it couldn't lead to success; it had, for many people. But not, according to my friends, for someone like me. Combining my instability and delusions of grandeur with interning was a recipe for catastrophe, being blacklisted from the industry, and possible criminal charges. Given that interns have to eat heaping loads of shit on a daily basis, everyone who knew me assured me I would snap within a week and assault some midlevel talent agent when they screamed at me for not getting the right amount of cream in their coffee.

No matter. I was already at work on my first novel and all I needed was a menial job to pay the rent for my studio apartment and the minimum on my credit cards while I completed a few spec scripts along with my very own *This Side of Paradise.*[2]

Come college graduation, the only real work experience I had to speak of, outside of manning the register at a Mrs. Field's Cookies branch and a hectic but satisfying run in the world of profes-

---

2   The title of F. Scott Fitzgerald's first published novel. And if you had to actually read this footnote to find out this bit of information, shame on you.

sional wrestling, was as a desk clerk at a Bed and Breakfast. Thus, I went to a job fair and filled out an application for the Pitz.

The Pitz is a chain of luxury hotels, and claims to offer impeccable service not to mere guests, but to "ladies and gentlemen." The branch I wound up at was in Marina Del Rey, and I must admit the outside looked impressive. Stone lions guarded the circular entrance, and the grounds were sprawling with a beautiful pool, tennis courts, and a hot tub that provided a picturesque view of the sunset over the ocean. I'd often dreamt of staying at such a hotel, although my course in life was already making it apparent to me that I might not ever be the type who could casually fork over $300 a night for a place to lay my head. Fortunately my time working at the Pitz obliterated any and all of my notions that such a hotel had anything remotely to do with luxury.

The first inklings came during the three day Orientation Period, during which time we recent hires were given twenty Credos to memorize. Examples:

When responding to a guest's thank you, always reply 'my pleasure.' Do not reply 'you're welcome' or any other variation.

Whenever a guest asks you for directions, always escort them personally to their destination.

Never smile too widely at a guest or laugh unless they tell a joke and laugh at it first.

Never, under ANY circumstances, call a guest by their first name.

In spite of the somewhat draconian nature of these and the sixteen other similarly themed doctrines, I memorized them to the best of my ability. I honestly felt a stubborn desire to be a good employee, and meeting the General Manager of our hotel only inspired me. The manager, Jeffrey, gave us new employees a talk on how he had started as a desk clerk at the San Diego Pitz many years ago and worked his way up to his current position as General Manager. With his lime green suit, singsong voice and eyes that glazed over as soon as they found yours, he was an inspiration. If this guy could become a manager of a Pitz hotel, then anyone could.

On the third day, as part of our Graduation, we were shown a video featuring, purportedly, the founder of the Pitz chain. His cheeks were tight against his face and his head darted this way and that as though he were expecting an attack from somewhere as he harangued us with a diatribe about how lucky we new employees were to be entrusted to the Pitz family. "You have been chosen as special people," he assured us, eyes straining so valiantly it was as though he were trying to see whoever might be on the other side of the camera. "Now swear to yourself that you will act accordingly."

The only thing I swore to myself was that I would never get addicted to whatever kind of meds this guy was obviously on.

My first day on the job I was issued a uniform of blue shorts and a white polo shirt with a Pitz insignia. When I wondered aloud whether this was proper attire for those who manned the front desk, I was informed I'd been reassigned to the fitness center, the reason given was because they were "full up" at the front desk.

The real reason, which would make itself known in short order, was that the fitness center was a dumping ground. There was only one other fitness center attendant, a man named George. He was around 35, pudgy, and had a smile that seemed permanently smudged. On my first day working with him he announced with pride that he'd been at the Pitz for thirteen years, working his way up from parking attendant to his current position of, as he put it, commander of the fitness center. Years of service at the Pitz had imparted on him a facial twitch that managed to make him look as though he was constantly either fulfilling a guest's request or anticipating a potential one, even when he was standing all alone behind the fitness center's counter. So imbued was this man with the Pitz' list of Credos that if a guest were to have told him they were plotting the destruction of the planet, George would've dutifully asked, "How can I assist you with that?"

In his quest to "set me up for success," George grandly revealed that fitness center attendants were required to take care of not only the fitness center, the locker rooms, and the terrace just outside, but also the entire pool area. One hundred and ten chairs all had to have towels folded on them just so. We fitness center attendants also had to make sure towels, robes, soap and mouthwash were available at the fitness center desk at all times. In addition to these duties we were responsible for taking massage appointments, washing down the exercise machines, and keeping the floor vacuumed and windows washed.

He told me all this with a pride so blatant it made me ashamed to feel angry that I'd been stuck with this position. Here was a man, at least ten years my senior, who felt *honored* that so much responsibility was placed squarely on his shoulders. He went on to tell me he'd been working several double-shifts, fourteen hours at a time, because they couldn't find anyone who was suitable for the position of his fitness center attendant partner.

"But now you're here, big guy!" he exclaimed jovially, placing a meaty hand on my shoulder. "This is gonna be great!"

I had the sneaking suspicion I'd encountered another psychopath, but soon learned that George was not only sane but brilliantly devious. By keeping the fitness center understaffed and undersupplied, George was able to work double shifts and collect massive amounts of overtime pay. I was working seventy hours a week myself, and when I mentioned to George that if we hired a third fitness attendant we could knock our workweek down to a reasonable forty hours a week, he just laughed and told me to enjoy the "overtime gravy."

Given the choice between overtime gravy and a little bit of sleep, I was ready to take the sleep.

For my first three weeks with George I actually tried to be a model employee. I was courteous to every guest. When one called me pathetic because I wasn't wearing a watch so I could tell him what time it was, I didn't point out that he was equally pathetic because *he* wasn't wearing a watch. I simply said that I'd be happy to call the Concierge Desk to have someone assist him with the current time.

While placing towels on pool chairs, a female guest asked me where the bathrooms were. When I insisted on escorting her there she called me a goddamn pervert and marched off in a huff. I called out that I was sorry for not meeting her needs.

Day after day of this kind of encounter with others can take a toll on one's psyche. I began to feel personally responsible when guests glared at me because there weren't any clean robes available. My wearing a nametag became a license for others to squint at my chest, then address a question to me with a sarcastic, "Okay, Shawn?" at the end.

The courts have named it *Battered Wife Syndrome.* At the Pitz, it was just part of the gig. Oddly I did feel some happiness after these exchanges, if only because the people giving me shit were so obviously miserable.

While being spoken down to was at least tolerable, being complimented was agonizing. One day a guest informed me, "Shawn, you're one hell of a fitness center attendant." When I found myself blushing with pride I became horrified. So maybe I wasn't a genius. Perhaps five would get you, well, a million that I wasn't ever going to invent a cure for cancer. But I was familiar with the films of Eric Rohmer, I knew where and when Wolfgang Amadeus Mozart had been born, I could name all of

Tennessee Williams' plays in chronological order and discuss the broader themes of each and every one. I was writing five hundred words a day on a novel that was going to win the National Book Award, for chrissakes, and here I was being complimented on my *fitness attendant* skills?

My third week on the job, the hotel had a surprise audit and found out they'd been paying George almost $60,000 a year for the past two years to run the fitness center. The Pitz immediately promoted George to a new position. Fitness Center Manager. "We've created a new position just for you, George!" Shane Browne, the Rooms Manager and our direct superior informed George one day. This meant that George would now be on straight salary, which I heard was somewhere in the $30,000 range. Most strategically on the part of the Pitz, George's promotion would mean no more overtime pay. He immediately hired another fitness center attendant, Freddy, and from then on we saw George only in passing and in departmental meetings.

Freddy was a force of nature. He stood a few inches above six feet and weighed around two hundred and thirty pounds, was gay, and seemed to take a delight in flaunting any convention. He and his lover Leo would cruise out on missions they called "phobe-bashing" in which they'd go into a bar and begin to flirt outrageously with one another. If anyone looked at them with the slightest askance, Freddy and Leo would immediately demand to know what the hell they were staring at, hadn't they ever seen two men in love before?

Though he was around my age, Freddy was obviously a great deal wiser. He classified the guests of the Pitz as a "damn bunch of rich flies that are staying temporarily at the same piece of shit." When I asked him why he'd taken a job at this place he apparently didn't care for, serving people he seemingly loathed, he answered, "Slumming."

Still Freddy deferred to guests, as did I, and we always saw that their needs were met. Or at least the *appearance* of their needs.

Marty and Julio were two of our best guests. Regulars who stayed on the top floor as VIP guests, they came out from Vegas almost every weekend, and it was rumored our hotel manager Jeffrey owed them a severe amount of money. The top floor had an open bar, and so the two of them, good souls that they were, took to bringing me down cocktails throughout Saturday and Sunday afternoon.

Freddy and I worked together on the weekends, handling the demands of all guests in the fitness center and pool area. The Pitz handbook insisted we work-ers refer to the hotel guests as "ladies and gentlemen," and the number of ladies and gentlemen always tripled on weekends because on Saturday and Sunday anyone who wandered in off the Marina and ordered a drink at the cabana was classified as a guest. One Sunday Marty asked for a robe and I didn't have any available; they were all in the laundry room.

"No robe?!" he exclaimed. "I've brought you drinks all day and you don't have a robe for me?"

There was no arguing with this kind of concrete logic. "I'll be right back, Marty!" I answered immediately. I hurried into the bowels of the hotel and into the damp heat of the laundry room, where there were four massive dryers and two medium sized washers. Five wheeled carts of dirty laundry and linen were lined up at the washers. "I need a robe!" I cried.

Four people were always on duty in the laundry room. All were Hispanic and all were always hustling and sweating. The Senior man, a guy in his fifties, neat pencil moustache, shrugged at me. "No washers."

"What can we do?" I asked.

He gave me another shrug. This time it was a slower, more conspiratorial one.

"Two dryers open, mi hermano," he smiled.

Five minutes later I had a freshly dried and neatly folded robe in hand and was carrying it out to Marty, who thanked me and spent the rest of the afternoon lounging by the pool in a fluffy unwashed robe.

It didn't take long for an unspoken pact to develop between the laundry room crew and me. I would drop off a load of dirty towels and robes, tell them I needed it "right away," and leave before I could see them stuffing the used linen in the dryer. With my view of the way corporate hotels were run growing more compromised by the day, I figured if I never actually saw any transgression, there was no transgression. Hedge-fund managers and mortgage loan officers have made fortunes using this philosophy; all I used it for was to keep the ladies and gentlemen staying at the Pitz reasonably happy and to keep the laundry crew supplied with the energy drinks we stocked in the fitness center.

As months passed I learned that the Pitz charged their ladies and gentlemen not for luxury but simply for its simulacrum. The hotel was like a beat up automobile with a fresh coat of paint and an inside doused with a "new car" smell. Fresh out of college, this was the first time that I saw behind the scenes of an operation that purported itself as top of the line, but in reality was as human and messy as the making of a Chorizo sausage or a Congressional Spending Bill.

Rats. Being so near the Marina, the Pitz had a problem with the creatures, some of which were as big as those dogs people carry around in their purses. They were often seen darting through the basement hallways, and had been spotted on occasion in the employee changing rooms as well as the cafeteria. Though there'd been no sightings upstairs (that were allowed to be reported anyway), there were banquet halls on the basement level, and it wasn't uncommon for an employee to have to go on "rodent duty" to chase away any rats from the open doors of an ongoing banquet.

Supplies were another matter. Managers got bonuses if they were able to run their respective departments under budget every month. This meant that all department managers guarded their budgeted amenities such as miniature shampoos, soaps, and razor blades with a vengeance. More than once George got into a scuffle with the Manager of Housekeeping over a missing gross of shampoos he thought she'd stolen. She would turn around and accuse him of stealing her washcloths. The people who were doing most of the stealing were actually the ladies and gentlemen we hosted, particularly on the aforementioned weekends when anyone off the street who had the price of an eight dollar beer could have access to our robes, towels, washrooms, etc.

Not to say there weren't some goings-on with the staff as well. The Pitz liked to think of all their employees as a "family," and it was a family all right. A dysfunctional one. It was rumored one of our night managers had made off with the painting that hung in our front lobby and replaced it with a picture perfect copy. Supposedly the painting had surfaced in the underground art market and fetched about $75,000. The Pitz, not wanting to admit that the painting which greeted all guests entering the lobby was a fraud, never acknowledged the theft, nor did they fire the manager. They simply proceeded to transfer the thief to a different hotel every month, figuring he would soon grow tired of never seeing his wife and three children and quit. Fourteen years after he allegedly stole the painting, this dogged employee was still a happy member of the Pitz family.

Life in the fitness center did have its bonuses. Due to the simple fact that our department was so far down on the ladder, we had license to easily coast under the radar and run wild. One of the perks was our massage therapists: all were in their forties, vibrant, sprightly, and constantly sexually harassing me. They were wonderful. Even better, the chefs and bartenders in the restaurant were in love with them, which meant there was a constant stream of food and cocktails being smuggled down from the dining room, which the therapists would share with us attendants in their massage rooms.

I had a particular crush on one of the therapists, a nimble looking lady named Clarissa. She had a wonderful way of staring at you as though she'd like nothing more than to have wild uninhibited times. She was a bit plump and always had a string of her blonde bangs dangling over her left eye. She was British, and her accent combined with her light attitude infused every word she spoke to me with a simmering sexuality.

One late afternoon she and I were sharing an early dinner of appropriated seafood fettucini alfredo in the massage room of the male locker room and the vibe was perfect. We were both giddy on screwdrivers and she confessed to me that she often fantasized about shagging someone in her massage room.

"Isn't that scandalous?" she asked, making *scandalous* sound like a ticket to heaven.

I was ready to take the trip. "It is," I agreed, thankful it was a Tuesday and things were always murderously slow in the fitness center on Tuesdays. Not to mention that it was George's day off and he wouldn't be lurking about making sure we attendants were keeping busy washing the windows or picking lint off the carpet.

Clarissa and I touched hands over our plates of fettucini. Then our lips were touching. And then our tongues. Her hands were caressing my blue shorts and my lips were gnawing on her neck when she suddenly burst out laughing.

"What the hell's so funny?" I sputtered romantically.

"That painting!" she hooted.

I turned to where she was pointing over my shoulder and gasped. There hung a portrait of the most hideous looking bird I'd ever seen. With a shaggy blue body and a long yellowed beak, it looked like the possible offspring of Big Bird and Oscar the Grouch. What made it really horrid was that whatever sadist had drawn the damn thing had done so as a frontal shot, and its two red eyes gazed accusingly at whoever happened to be unlucky enough to be looking back. Which at the moment happened to be me and a woman I was trying to seduce over a dinner of purloined pasta.

"Ignore it," I urged. "Let's get back to you and I…" I paused. "And your scandalous fantasy." I concluded, with what I hoped was a seductive purr.

Clarissa tried, but soon she was giggling again.

"I'm sorry, Shawn," she chuckled. "But I just can't do it with that bird staring at us."

Unfortunately, even when Clarissa and I got together after work that night she began to laugh whenever we began to get amorous. "That bird," she laughed. "That bird looked so *cross.*"

Clarissa claimed it was a sign of some sort, and we wound up agreeing to remain just good friends. *Just good friends.* Of all the three word combinations that suck, that one has to rank in the top ten. I did later learn that Clarissa was actually a year over fifty and had a son around my age, so that could've been the reason she didn't want to seal the deal. However, I felt certain that it wouldn't have mattered had we been able to be swept away in the moment in that massage room. Thus I vowed vengeance upon that damn bird.

The bird wasn't the only problem I had. Seasons had shifted and the days were growing rapidly shorter. Meanwhile Freddy was keeping up a constant campaign against the Pitz, along with its ladies and gentlemen. He was fond of opening the small complimentary bottles of soap, lotion and aftershave, and then - his phrase - *bestowing upon them* a symbolic drop of his urine. The purpose of this, as he explained, was to "piss on the rich morons who pretend to be what they are not." He also stole from the Pitz with reckless abandon. One night he managed to wear two robes and a towel stuffed in his crotch beneath his street clothes as he walked past hotel security. It was a talent to be admired.

Yet it was a talent I didn't possess. For reasons of my own, I was still mired in some lunatic desire to be a model employee. Sure, I cut corners by not washing towels when we were backed up. But I never stole. I still faithfully folded each and every towel perfectly as I laid them out on the poolside chairs every morning at 6:00 A.M.

This is where Christmas Day of that year found me at six in the morning: laying out carefully folded towels on one hundred and ten poolside chairs. I looked into the sky grown pink with the sunrise. I wasn't looking for Santa's sleigh but instead for an answer. My novel was finished, no agents wanted it, and I had a college degree in Radio, Television and Film. I began to ponder where I might be in five years. If I'd taken the internship with that entertainment agency, I'd most likely be climbing the ladder of Hollywood's young turks. I would've controlled my temper and swallowed as much shit as they could've thrown at me, worked the eighteen hour days without complaint. I'd be growing into an agent who felt important enough to not return phone calls (when, I asked myself for the umpteenth time since graduation day, was the last time you heard of a fuck-ing *writer* not returning a phone call in Hollywood?). Instead here I was, an "art-ist" who'd chosen the supposed high road of creation and now was spending Christ-mas morning laying out towels, wondering what it would be like to be out at this pool as a guest instead of a worker.

"Shawn! What the hell are you doing?"

"Who knows? Wasting my life?" I answered myself.

"No!" this voice, now definitely not my own, came loud and crisp. "You're not wasting your life, you're wasting time! You're standing around and not doing a damn thing."

I turned and saw Shane Browne, the hotel's Rooms Manager who'd gleefully informed George that the hotel was giving him a promotion and cutting his annual salary in half. Shane's nickname amongst us hotel employees was "the fist." The origin of the moniker was murky, but from what I could gauge, not only was Shane constantly scowling as if he had a fist up his ass, but he acted like the kind of guy who lived to stick his fist up other people's asses and watch them squirm. He could often be heard berating the housekeeping staff, threatening to "yank away your green cards and send you all back to fucking Mexico." He also didn't hesitate to make fun of Freddy every time my co-worker was out of earshot, calling him a "jacked up King's Road fairy."

On this Christmas morning, Shane's angered expression seemed clear evidence Santa had neglected to visit him last night. "What is your job at this hotel?" Shane barked at me.

"Damned if I know," I replied, before I could opine otherwise.

A confused look infiltrated his frozen sneer. In that moment he looked almost human, and I thought this might be an opening for a bonding of sorts.

"Look, Shane," I began, "You're work-ing on Christmas Day, and you probably don't want to be, just like me. Now why don't we agree to be friends, comrades if you will? It's either that or we become enemies. Your call."

I was rather proud of that last line, which I'd stolen from the latest episode of my favorite show on cable. It didn't, however, provoke the reaction I was look-ing for. Instead of swallowing nervously as he realized, regardless of how high above me he might be in the Pitz peck-ing order I was nonetheless a person to be reckoned with, Shane shook his head as though trying to dismiss a circling fly and shouted, "You're not wearing your nametag!"

I looked down at my chest, and saw the space over my right nipple was bare.

"Sorry," I shrugged. "I think it fell into the toilet."

"What?"

I'd been up late last night on Christmas Eve, having a few vodka and tonics, still wearing my Pitz shirt because I knew I'd be too buzzed to remember to put it on at 4:30 in the morning when I had to leave for work. So I'd been tottering above the toilet, relieving myself, and the pin that held my nametag had somehow become loose and then there'd been a splash.

There my name had been, emblazoned on imitation copper, bobbing up at me. Though it would've been easy enough to put my hand in a bowl of my own piss to retrieve it, my buzz told me such an action would go against a principle of sorts. Following this logic, I'd flushed the toilet with a flourish and strode victoriously from the bathroom before collapsing onto my mattress and box spring for three hours of haphazard unconsciousness.

Upon hearing this story, Shane tilted his head to one side, his glasses picking up some sun from the sky and instilling his eyes with a predatory glint. "You would dare drink just hours before you had to report to work?" he asked, seemingly baffled.

Well, yes. When someone's in a city like Los Angeles, with no family to spend Christmas with, ready to report to a minimum-wage job at 5:30 in the morning, what better time to drink?

This explanation, reasonable as it sounded to me, only made his head cock another couple degrees to the right. More sun infiltrated his eyes and fanned an increasing predatorily like glow. He started to speak several times, then snapped, "I'm writing you up!"

He stalked away. I stared back at the rising sun, wondering idly (and admittedly, a bit drunkenly) if I'd just fucked up by being totally frank. Then I decided to hell with it and went back to laying out towels.

Later that day, Shane stomped into the fitness center and presented me with my write-up. Scanning it briefly, I learned that *on the morning of December 25th, Shawn was seen in the pool area in violation of Credo Number 3 (wearing a nametag at all time). For this violation Shawn has been issued this write-up. Two more may result in further discipline and/or termination.*

I laughed. Shane fumed. Just then a lady guest padded out of the locker room. "Thank you for the towel," she waved.

I waved back. "You're welcome."

"It was *his pleasure,* ma'am." Shane intoned.

She walked out, and Shane turned to me. "That's another write-up," he said.

"For what?"

"You didn't respond properly to a guest's thank you."

"I said you're welcome."

"You're supposed to say it was your pleasure!"

I stared at this creature before me. I knew that Shane held a Bachelors Degree, the same as me. His was presumably in Hotel Management whereas mine was in Butt Picking, but nonetheless I had managed to complete studies for a university of higher learning, just like he had.

It occurred to me that maybe it would help to explore this common ground.

"What made you want to major in Hotel Management, Shane?" I asked him.

"What the hell are you talking about?"

"You have a college degree, right?" I went on. "In hotel management?"

"I have a college degree," Shane snapped. "But it's none of your damn business what my major was!"

He turned on his heel and strode out of the fitness center.

I called in a few favors with some people in Personnel and was able to get a peek at Shane's employment file. I was stunned to see that he had a college degree all right, a college degree from the very same Cal State system I'd graduated from.

His degree was in Anthropology.

Anthro-fucking-*pology?!* And this guy was questioning my work ethic?

When I'd been in college there'd been a running joke amongst the RTVF students that our degrees were going to be about as useful in the real world as ones in Anthropology, which was defined by the college guide as "the scientific study of the origin, the behavior, and the physical, social and cultural development of humans."

So a guy who'd taken classes about the evolution of silverware in human dining was, according to the hierarchy of the Pitz, authorized to bully his workers, many of whom sweated more in a day than he had in, judging by his birth date and the year he wrote down as his graduation, all eight years it had taken him to finish college.

I closed Shane's file. It was at this instant that I decided to declare war on the Pitz. Total war.

It's true that when I'd first joined the "Pitz family," I'd flirted with brief fantasies of following Jeffrey's example and climbing the corporate ladder to General Manager. It stood to reason that if this position could be attained by a goof who dressed in suits that made him look like a human lollipop, then surely a person of my reasonable intelligence could pull it off. Horatio Alger come to life. The bourgeois part of me that I always did my best to deny had in fact been intoxicated at the idea of becoming one with the world that the Pitz promised, one of luxury, power, and wholly undeserved entitlement.

Now, realizing there was no way I was going to accomplish this, I knocked my goal down several notches to the rank of saboteur. I began to steal robes and towels at a rate that rivaled even Freddy, pitching them into the bushes in the Marina and retrieving them after I strolled out of the work area. Seven was the record number of little shampoo bottles I was able to fit into my crotch and not create a suspicious bulge. George was at his wits end trying to figure out where all his inventory was going. Searching for a way to justify my internal demotion and the actions it demanded, I compared myself to Robin Hood and made sure to drop off the robes and towels at the Salvation Army and give out the little shampoo and soap bottles to homeless people.

I stopped wearing my nametag. When people thanked me I loudly declared that they were welcome. I openly sneered at

Shane in the hallway. One night I crowned all by flaunting the rule that we fitness attendants had to stay in the fitness center/pool area, strolling through the front lobby and into the lounge while still in my work uniform of blue shorts and white Pitz shirt so that I could make out with a guest that had been hitting on me in the fitness center. Whenever George tried to good naturedly quiz me on the Twenty Credos of the Pitz (in his seemingly endless attempt to set me up for success), I snarled and quoted what I referred to as the Twenty-First Credo: "I can't assist you with that at this time, so piss off."

I was looking to get fired. That much was obvious. The only problem was the Pitz *wouldn't* fire me. I'd been assigned to a job nobody but a wide-eyed college graduate with a dream of treading financial waters while they wrote the Great American Novel would want. However, just as the Pitz didn't want to get rid of me, I certainly wasn't about to leave voluntarily. If I quit, it would mean that a corporate run entity had achieved a victory over my rebellious and free-thinking spirit. On a more practical note, it also meant that I wouldn't be able to collect unemployment insurance.

Thus, the Pitz and I were locked in a stalemate.

But at last came the hour of reckoning. It was a Monday, which just happened to be my day off. George had chosen this day to hold our departmental meeting at 9:00 A.M. in the morning. I assumed I'd be excused from attending, but when I brought this up to him the day before, he informed me with the ponderous delivery of a boss who takes their job way too seriously that attendance was mandatory.

"Mandatory," he repeated, evidently proud of himself for using a polysyllabic word. The only thing that marred the effect was he pronounced the first part of the word as *"main."*

That Sunday evening, as I was picking up towels scattered around the pool area by our visiting ladies and gentlemen, I noticed a funny smell. I looked down and saw that the towel in my hand was stained brown.

I dropped the towel in disgust. The towel fell open, revealing two small pieces of dung. Immediately I remembered there'd been some twenty-something VIP guest out there today, with the kind of dog you could mistake for a rat running loose in the halls of the Pitz, and she'd been heard complaining loudly that there was no place for her dog to "doo-doo" in private.

I'd been bitten on the hand that day by a six year old kid as I tried to help him onto a bicycle while his parents laughed and jokingly assured me he didn't have rabies. At least half a dozen people had looked at me with sympathy as I rushed around, shirt soaked with sweat, and said: "You're really doing a good job, young man." I appreciated their wishes and thanked them, but at the same time wondered why the hell I wasn't doing something more productive, like skipping a rock along some picturesque pond in the middle of nowhere while pondering how the word *ecclesiastical* had earned its definition. Then just as my shift was ending the hotel's head of Engineering, Peter Rodriguez, a fat man who wore a wig that would make a drag queen scream in horror, had charged into the fitness center, coked out of his mind as usual, shouting that all the spent towels laying by the pool were freaking him out. It was fairly well known by the staff that he knew little about engineering and the reason he held the position he did was that he and Jeffrey shared a special friendship of some sorts. Nothing wrong with that, but did it really give him any right to holler at me about towels while he was wired to the gills?

I stared at the two turds nestled within the Pitz towel in my hand and determined, quite literally, that I didn't need this shit anymore. My thoughts raced ahead to the meeting the next morning, and my lips found a grin.

Mandatory, my ass. I'd show them *main*-datory.

The next morning, fueled by that exhilaration an upcoming confrontation always seems to bring, I flew out of bed at 6:00 A.M. and within ten minutes was enjoying a cocktail. Of course, when one has a cocktail at that hour nothing will do but to have another. And then perhaps just one more. Thus fortified, I biked over to the Pitz, headed into the fitness center and went directly to the male massage room. There I stood face to face with the painting that featured the animal I most hated at the Pitz. More than the kiss-ass chain of command that encouraged mediocrity, more than Shane's arrogance or Peter's coke-fueled paranoia, more than the string of "ladily and gentlemanly" crap that held this overpriced house of cards upright...

It was the damn bird that had cost me my amorous adventure with Clarissa.

I snatched the painting of this horrendous looking monster off the wall and proceeded to the conference room, where our departmental meeting was being held. George, Freddy, and all the massage therapists were there. I was surprised to see Shane present as well. He cut his eyes at me as I sauntered into the room. "What's that you got there?" he demanded, staring at the painting.

"What's that you *have* there is the correct grammar, Mister Anthropology," I replied, slamming the painting down on the table. Then I sat.

Shane's uncomfortable look was already making it worth it that I'd had to wake up so early on my day off.

Shane turned his scowl from me to George, who jumped to his feet, clapped his hands together and stated, "All right, ladies and gentlemen, we're very happy to be here and address all our constructive input-"

"I'm not happy to be here," I snorted.

George looked at me as if I were growing wings.

"It's my day off," I pointed out. "Who the hell arranged this meeting on my day off?"

"When you're a member of the Pitz family, Shawn," Shane spoke crisply. "You adapt to a—"

"Shane!" I interrupted. "Do you realize that when you use the words 'Pitz family,' you sound like a total asshole?"

Silence.

I ran my finger up and down the painting while staring around the table. "You want constructive input at this meeting?

I've got some input, and it's constructive as can be."

At this point Freddy shifted in his seat, aimed his rear end at me, and hooted, "Baby, give me your input!"

"Maybe later," I laughed, then regained my indignation. I had, after all, come to this meeting on a mission. "We've got no towels, we've got no robes, because this goddamn hotel is too cheap to buy any! What's more, the guests rob this place all the time. And I've been robbing this place blind, too! But all you managers are too damn busy with your noses up in the air to notice."

Sweet confession. I could feel my soul being cleansed with every word.

George's mouth was opening and closing soundlessly. He looked as astounded as Dr. Frankenstein, when the good doctor realized his monster had eclipsed his control. It *was* George who had told me from day one in what had sounded like an honest tone that he wanted to set me up for success. Well, my idea of success was calling out nonsense when I saw it. That was one of the many reasons my friends had advised me against interning in the entertainment industry. Given my mindset, maybe it would turn out I would be no good to *any* industry. To hell with it. I could always sleep on the beach.

A person like George, on the other hand, had mouths to feed. He wasn't a bad sort at all. But he had to play the game, and for the time being, I didn't. As I stared at him, I wondered if he might have been like me once. His head was jerking with such vehemence that it was impossible to tell whether he was shaking his head or nodding rapidly.

Choosing to believe the latter, that he wanted to revisit those old days when he'd had nothing to lose, I went on, "To make matters worse, the other day I went into the male massage room…"

I paused and glanced over at Clarissa. Her eyes were frightened and she was frantically making a *cut* motion with her left hand.

"To pleasure myself," I continued. "And I couldn't even get a hard on… because this damn painting is so ugly!"

I held up the guilty painting with one hand while with my other hand I mimicked shaking a limp dick.

"Sir, that's inappropriate!" George exploded.

"No shit," I answered. "This whole damn hotel is inappropriate! You have rats running through the hall while Citigroup's national officers and directors are meeting in one of the ballrooms!"

Little did I know that in a few years, America's financial bubble would burst and this analogy would prove fairly accurate.

Freddy was howling in laughter, George was on his feet looking ready to burst, and the massage therapists were all caught between looks ranging from shock to approval. Shane was sitting back, a crooked smile on his face, as though confident he'd driven me to this self-destructive meltdown. But I had a few words to say yet.

"And you Shane, you smug little son of a bitch," I told him. His smile wavered a bit but remained intact. "You threaten to yank our janitorial staff's green cards, you mock homosexuals—"

"He *what?*" Freddy barked, rising to his feet.

Faced with an aforementioned "phobe-basher," Shane was now backing up in his seat. "This direction is not how ladies and gentlemen conduct themselves-" he began.

"Oh, what the hell would you know about being a gentleman?" I demanded. "You use your position of authority to bully people, you don't have the slightest idea of how to deal with a customer, and you don't even know that we haven't washed a freakin' towel in months!"

Silence, save for Freddy's chuckles and George's labored breathing. Shane faced George. "Is this true, George?"

"George didn't know a damn thing about it," I said quickly. "Nobody did but me. And you call yourself a *manager.* You couldn't manage a cup of warm piss!"

As excited titters leaked from the massage therapists, Shane rose to his feet. "That's *enough,* Shawn!" he commanded.

His tone frightened me, because it made me feel for the first time in my life that I might actually be capable of committing murder in front of witnesses. It was then and there that it flashed before me the wonder of menial jobs; they were providers of the luxury that accompanies the potentiality of plunging from the bottom rung of a ladder. Lose a menial job and one could simply ask oneself, *Well, that wasn't so bad now, was it?*

I made a wild vow to myself that, if necessary, I would work menial jobs for the rest of my life. Answer phones in an office, run a mop along a floor, even stand out in the street dressed in a ridiculous costume with a cheesy arrow sign that said "$2.00 CAR WASH." True, these occupations might not provide potential for those relentlessly positive holiday letters some families send out (We had some cheers and some jeers this year… Our nephew Bartholomew was appointed to a top level management position at ICM, while our dog Puddles got ran over by a car and is now in doggie heaven). But working jobs such as this would ensure that if a snotnose boss like Shane gave me crap I could tell him to shove his job up his pockmarked ass.

I actually did one better with Shane, telling him to shove the entire fitness center up his ass. Then, for added effect, I held up the painting in my hands, the painting that had prevented me from making wild love to a beautiful woman, and slammed my fist through that bird's ugly yellow beak. I withdrew, then tossed the painting onto the table.

"It was my pleasure, asshole." I said to Shane. Then I tipped my hat to George, gave a thumbs-up to Freddy, blew a kiss to the massage therapists, and left the Pitz.

I walked out of the meeting, passed the hallways where rats were laying somewhere in wait, and into the sunshine of the pool area.

No longer an employee, I lay down on one of the guest chairs. It was mid morning and the sun was well into the sky.

I ordered a vodka-tonic from Marilyn, who worked morning shifts as waitress for the pool area. I contemplated the sun. Well, I was no longer a member of the Pitz family. Technically I was a guest, being that I'd just ordered a drink and could afford to pay for it. But I didn't feel like one. I certainly didn't feel like a gentleman in any sense of the word, as most gentlemen didn't go around fisting paintings of birds. All I was, for better or for worse, was my own person.

I decided I could live with that.

A PIECE OF EVIDENCE AS TO WHY SHAWN HAS NOT YET "MADE IT" AS A SCREENWRITER

```
                    RICHARD
          I think you need help. We can work
          together, and help you out. Hell, Jeff.
          We're all a little crazy.

                    JEFF
          Ever since that day, people have treated
          me like I'm nuts. Like there's something
          wrong with me. Everyone except you.
          You've always treated me like a person.

                    RICHARD
          Jeff, I've treated a lot of people. A lot
          of my patients don't want to be helped.
          It's like they've crossed over an edge,
          and decided they don't want help. And if
          somebody doesn't want help, you can't
          really do a lot for them.

                    JEFF
          What about me? You think you can do a lot
          with me?

                    RICHARD
          All these years, I've watched you teeter
          on that edge. But somehow you've managed
          to stay on it. I get the feeling you
          want to come back, you want to get
          better. And I can help you with that.

                    JEFF
          The thing is, I don't feel sick.

                    RICHARD
          But, Jeff. You can't go on like this.

                    JEFF
          Why not?

                    RICHARD
          Because you're too good for this kind
          of life.

                    JEFF
          You actually think I'm a good person?

                    RICHARD
          I think everybody has a little bit of
          both good and bad in them.

                    JEFF
          You ever have evil thoughts?

                    RICHARD
              (nods slowly)
          Yeah. I'd say everybody does.
```

One of the many pages of questionable attempts at the art of screenwriting found in Shawn Michals' apartment. My apologies to any of his screenwriting teachers who might be embarrassed by this.
- B.P

KICKING HOMOPHOBIA

Before the age of the Internet, personal phone lines were the way teenagers communicated in confidence to the outside world, away from the prying eyes of their parents. When I was around thirteen years old, I was blessed enough to have one of these private phone lines in my room. This was my secure link to others, upon which I could speak without fear of intrusion or judgment.

Unless, of course, Mom was outside my room eavesdropping on me. One Saturday afternoon I was talking to a buddy of mine and signed off by saying, "See you, sexy."

Innocent enough, I presumed, until I walked out of my room and came face to face with my mother's flaring eyebrows. "Who were you talking to just now?" she demanded.

"Sebastian," I replied. Sebastian was my best friend in eighth grade. We'd bonded over a mutual hatred of our algebra teacher and a mutual love of the Rambo movies.

"If anyone had been listening to you right then," my mother went on, "they would have thought you were a 'homosexual.'"

She brought her fingers up as mock quo-
tations to emphasize the word *homosexual.*
I knew a few things about homosexuals.
From what I could discern, most of them
seemed fairly well off, had great taste
in clothes, and were impeccably neat.
If my mom was worried that I was one of
these chosen few she was bound to be disappointed, being that she and I weren't
that well off, I had horrendous taste in
clothes, and my room looked like a sci-
ence experiment.

"I'm not," I assured my mother.

"If I find out you are," she drawled.
"I'll disown you so fast it'll make you
shit your pants."

She marched off into the kitchen while
I stifled the urge to break into a verse
from Culture Club's "Karma Chameleon" and
then ask her for makeup tips. Given the
volatile relationship between us disown-
ment would've been a blessing, soiled
pants be damned.

In spite of my efforts to put her
accusation out of my mind, it didn't
take long for my relationship with Sebastian to deteriorate. My mother's comment
turned acts that previously were just
two best friends fooling around with
each other into two best friends who
were literally fooling around with each
other. If a headlock were prolonged even
a little bit, I'd find myself squirm-

ing. Chest bumps, bear hugs… any physical contact was subject to being considered foreplay. The weight room was even worse, given that when one performs squats (a technique that involves a bar across one's back and a movement true to the exercise's name) one usually needs a spotter, whose job it is to squat down with the lifter, arms locked around the other's chest.

Mom's remark rendered this all too much for me to take. Every time I performed a squat, Sebastian's arms holding me tight, his breath on my neck, I heard my mother sneering "homosexual."

I informed Sebastian I wanted to work out on my own, and also put an end to our weekly *Dungeons and Dragons* sessions. Given my newly altered worldview, two boys whispering excitedly over battling imaginary monsters just seemed a bit *too* bonding.

One afternoon the summer before we were due to start high school, Sebastian called me and asked if I wanted to go to the movies that night. I stammered that I didn't think we should hang out anymore.

"Why not?" he asked, and to my ears his confusion sounded like the kind of emotion a jilted lover might display.

"I just… I just don't think we should see each other anymore."

"See each other?" he responded. "What the hell… are you some kind of fag or something?"

I saw my opportunity and went for it. "I'm not a fag!" I told him. "You're the fag!"

Thus began my age of homophobia.

Thankfully Sebastian and his family moved away that Christmas, so I was in high school without anyone who could unjustly accuse me of being anything other than heterosexual. Besides, I wasn't homosexual at all, and I proved it by dutifully referring to anything that wasn't considered cool as being the antithesis to cool: gay.

Hence, though I secretly liked a few New Kids On the Block songs, I announced to all who would listen that the group was "a bunch of homos." (Even though they were most likely shagging more women in one night than I ever would in two lifetimes). Meanwhile, getting good grades was for "queers who couldn't find a date on Friday nights." As far as *Dungeons and Dragons* went, I went so far as to burn my Players Manual, all the modules, and even my characters, including Beezle, my beloved Level 8 Thief who was part Elf and part Halfling.

By midway through Freshman year my straight personality was firmly in place, and I'd found a group of friends who shared my beliefs. We all liked to lift weights, smoke pot, and chase girls.

The Studs. This was our self appointed moniker, and even more amazing than the fact that we conned ourselves into believing this was that we were able to con the female population of our high school into believing it as well. It was a testament to those countless positive thinking manuals that expound the first step to "being" it is to "say" it. As we moved through our high school career, my friends and I found ourselves to be in constant demand by girls. At parties, we began to declare ourselves to be gay, as this proclamation only seemed to fuel the opposite sex's attraction for us.

This led to what my friends and I magnanimously termed "sessioning," which involved us all masturbating together while watching porn. During these sessions, we'd always comment on the actresses and their ample bosoms but never on the actors or the considerable size of their members. When one of our group, *[3], made the mistake of voicing amazement over the size of Ron Jeremy's penis, he was harangued by taunts of being "a homo" for months.

The more we flaunted our supposed homosexuality, the more girls at our school

---

3   Name deleted at insistence of publisher's *and* author's lawyers.

seemed to desire us. I lost count of the number of girls who asked me if I was really gay. All I had to do was shrug, and that would elicit the response, "Well, I can convert you." I was only too happy to succumb.

The few times I actually made out with my male friends at parties? Well, I assured myself while trying to ignore the memories and receding alcohol level pounding in my head, I'd been A) Drunk B) Putting on a show for all the girls I hadn't yet had convert me to heterosexuality and C) Made a display out of slamming vodka from the bottle afterwards so as to fend off the taste of another man's saliva.

Mornings after these incidents I would be sure to call my friends before lunch to make sure they knew about the three hotties I'd made out with after the "bullshit kiss (insert name here) and I faked."

After high school, when I arrived in L.A. to train as a professional wrestler, I found myself in a whole new quandary. Our teacher insisted that shaving our legs and slathering on baby oil before matches was mandatory. At first I balked, but after a while I grew to like it. Emerging from a bathtub, my whole body shaved, I felt clean. I would look at myself in the mirror and admire my pure smooth skin free of unwanted hair. I flexed my thigh muscles, bounced my pectorals, and told myself that the art of physical exhibition extended back to the times of gladiators, and if two grown men donned costumes and pretended to grapple with one another, there was not a damn thing homoerotic about it.

This belief was tested when I saw on the front page of a tabloid that a very famous and active professional wrestler had allegedly once worked as a gay prostitute in Atlanta. I remember snatching the offending headline off the rack and reading it as I stalked from aisle to aisle, muttering "bullshit" to myself. I angrily tore up the magazine and left its pieces on top of some dog food bags in aisle seven.

In the checkout line, the clerk rang up the twenty-four pack of Bic razors I was buying and smiled. "You shave every day?" he asked.

His tone was a little too friendly for my taste. "What the hell is that supposed to mean?" I roared.

He bit his lip and continued ringing up my baby oil, plus the fingernail polish and black lipstick that were part of my wrestling gimmick. I paid and marched self-righteously out of the store.

When I got a job as a trainer at a local gym, one of my first clients was a man named Nathan. He was in his mid forties, worked as a hairdresser, and lived with a gentleman he referred to as a roommate. Though I prided myself in being able to smell a faggot from a mile away, these red flags managed to elude me. Mostly, I suppose, because even though I professed a hatred for homosexuals, I'd never yet met a person who was openly gay.

Nathan and I became friends. I regaled him with reports of the matches I was having every weekend. After I became the champion of a fairly popular independent promotion in San Diego, I would drive down there each weekend and wrestle both Saturday and Sunday night, then be back in time to open up the club on Monday morning at 6:00 A.M. Nathan would be the first member to arrive, always wearing a jovial smile. His first question would be, "Do you still have your belt?"

"Damn right I do!" I responded with a growl, and Nathan would applaud. These little exchanges between people always help make a Monday morning brighter.

It was on one of these Mondays when I discovered Nathan was a homosexual. All started innocently enough, with him leaning in closely to me over the counter and asking, "Pardon me, Shawn. But is that vodka on your breath?"

Though I'd showered just an hour before, there was a good chance all the vodka I'd lapped up over the weekend was probably still making its way out of my pores.

Nathan's tone, far from accusatory, was more on the side of conspiratorial. Could it be that we were brothers, he and I, and that the good humor he always seemed to be in was because he was also one of the cocktail clique?

"Probably," I admitted.

He nodded.

"I think I'm an alcoholic," I said.

He nodded again.

"You're the first person I've told that to," I said.

He nodded yet again.

"I guess I'm out of the closet." I said. "I'm an alcoholic."

"Thank you," he said.

"For what?"

"For trusting me enough to come out."

"You're an alcoholic too?" I asked, pleased at finding a fellow chosen one.

Nathan laughed. "No," he replied. "I'm gay."

He may as well as announced he was Godzilla. "You're what?" I asked.

"You mean you hadn't guessed?" he asked.

I'd certainly not. Fags were pansies who flounced about in skirts, who spoke in lisps, who spread AIDS, and were an over-all menace to society. Fags were people who weren't, well, *right*.

But here was this man, someone I considered a friend, someone who was courteous, friendly, and ready to accept me for who I was. And he was telling me that he was what my mother had once threatened to disown.

"I'm sorry," I blurted, then immediately suspected that was the wrong thing to have said.

Nathan laughed. He waved away my concerns, then headed off to finish his workout.

One Friday Nathan mentioned he had a doctor's appointment the next day for some tests because he had what he called "a bug of sorts."

That Monday morning I opened up the club and waited for Nathan to show up. I'd pushed the fact that he was gay to the farther reaches of my mind. The night before I'd sustained a blow to the head from a steel chair and had required four stitches. I was proud of the scar, and for some reason Nathan was the first person I wanted to see it.

But he didn't show up that day. He didn't come into the gym at all that week.

The next Monday, I asked a few of the regulars if they'd heard anything about Nathan. One of them, Teddy, mentioned that he got his hair cut at the salon where Nathan worked and that he had been hospitalized and was "very sick."

"Between you and me," Teddy said quietly, leaning over the counter and checking to make sure nobody was looking. "I think he's got that funny disease." He let his wrist go limp and wagged his hand back and forth in an exaggerated fashion.

"Funny?" I asked.

He mouthed the word, "AIDS."

This was right after AIDS had killed Rock Hudson, and the disease had been thrust into the public eye. Many people had already firmly stamped it as a gay disease. Preachers preached about how it was God's will that homosexuals were contracting the disease. One reverend, who would later be arrested with a male prostitute in his car, became well known for his sermons that this was God's vengeance upon homosexuals. Married people were immune to what he termed this "disease of the damned."

The next night I went to the local hospital. I gave the nurse on duty Nathan's name, and she asked if I was friend or family. I was taken by surprise. It was the first time I'd ever visited someone in a hospital, and I didn't know how this could be important. "I'm his…" I paused, surprised to find the word "son" on the tip of my tongue. Then again, having grown up without a father around, I'd spent most of my childhood and teenage years looking up to just about every adult male who'd seemed to have a genuine interest in me and my goals. "I'm his cousin," I told the nurse.

She gave me his room number and told me she was sorry.

The room's door was open slightly. I walked in and there was the smell of stale flesh battling with disinfectant. Nathan's body had grown painfully thin. His eyes were shut. Sores covered his face. I stood before his bed, terrified, afraid to even inhale.

"Are you the wrestler?"

The question caught me off guard. I found its source. A man was seated rigidly on a chair in the corner of the room. He looked to be in his mid-forties, with wide shoulders and a slight paunch. "I'm Martin," he said, rising to his feet. His voice was creaky, dampened by tears. "Nathan's roommate."

I nodded. Since I didn't trust myself to say anything, I did the next best thing. I took out the flask I'd brought along and had a swallow. Martin let out a slight chuckle. "Nathan mentioned you liked to drink," he said.

I nodded again. Then I tentatively offered him the flask.

He shook his head. "I'm all right," he said. "Thank you."

I was relieved he hadn't taken a drink, hadn't put his lips on my flask. Then I felt guilty for being relieved.

"I'd better go," I said. I had to get out of that room.

"He's dying," Martin said. "He's dying and I can't stop it."

With shame I remembered how in high school my friends and I used to refer to gay bashing as a "public service." Now a gay man was staring at me with tears in his eyes because he was going to lose his lover.

I was startled to find I both despised and feared this man and his dilemma. Not because he was gay, but because he was as powerless as I was, as we all are, to stop people we love from dying.

Two years ago, before I'd come out west to L.A., the person I'd been wouldn't have been afraid at all. He would've sneered at this grieving man the way a rich arrogant man may sneer at a homeless person. *Tough luck, fag.*

But now, confronted with the opportunity to not only bash a homosexual, but to really hurt one at a time when he was weakest, I didn't see a homosexual. I saw a human being, a human being who was losing someone he loved. I had desires I was sometimes embarrassed of, thoughts I often regretted, and had already lost count of how many stupid assumptions I'd made in my twenty years. I wasn't always proud of who I was. I simply was.

My voice cracked. As I hugged Martin, I found myself feeling like a human being. And for the first time in my life, not ashamed of it.

BIKING UNDER THE INFLUENCE

One of the truly thought provoking aspects of America is that to become this country's President, the sole requirements are to be a natural born citizen, have lived in this country for at least fourteen years, and be at least thirty-five years of age. These are the only concrete criteria set forth by the United States Constitution. One technicality our Founding Fathers didn't mention is that these days it also helps to have at least three hundred million dollars in ~~bribes~~ political contributions. But still, the potential for a poverty stricken dark horse with only, say, fifty million at their disposal does exist.

Liberty, long may she reign.

Employing this logic, upon entering college as a Freshman at age twenty-five I signed up for a Public Speaking class. Secure in my delusions of grandeur, I figured that when I ran for the office of the President of the United States ten years down the road I would at the very least have to know how to address a crowd with a smile, even if I was lying my ass off.

The first day of class, we were asked to relate a story that had impacted our lives. I volunteered eagerly, because I had a great one. It had happened just a few weeks ago. Some of my friends and I, after drinking at a Frat party all night, had decided it was the perfect time for a road trip to Vegas. I regaled the class with the recount of how we'd made numerous beer stops and toasted to everything we could think of as we made our way through the late night and early morning across the desert. Somehow during our journey I'd acquired a bullhorn, and spent much of my time bellowing out the driver's window about how we were going to Vegas to affirm everything that was right and true about the American Dream. Amongst many hazy promises, I swore that if elected President I would let the people of the Middle East slaughter one another in their Holy Crusades without the sacrifice of American lives, that marijuana and prostitution would be legalized and taxed accordingly, that our wonderful country would return to its roots and mind our own damn business unless forced to do otherwise. As I ranted and raved out the window I also made references to money, strippers, and the roll of the dice... a promise that to vote for me for President would be a vote for the potential that all would be overturned in a country driven mad by special interests and polarization.

I had to be pretty toasted to think I'd win on that kind of platform.

But my relation of this episode and my intoxicated Presidential agenda did manage to bring half the class to hysterical applause and leave the other half shaking their heads in bewilderment. Certainly a better response than the one I'd received when I'd actually been hollering this wishful rigmarole through a megaphone while driving to Vegas. Before we'd hit Death Valley, all my friends in the car had been snoozing away. Now, at least, I had an active audience, and what seemed like a draw between approval and disapproval. Good enough. Presidents had been elected on less than a majority of the popular vote.

I took my seat, secure in my Presidential prospects.

The very next speaker was a pale blonde young woman who looked as though she'd been placed on this earth for no other purpose than to suffer. As she started her speech she was almost already in tears. Soon she was weeping her way through a tale about how a few years ago she'd been on the phone with her friend, and her bulldog, Buster, had needed to go to the bathroom. Instead of hanging up with her friend and walking Buster she'd told her dog "not to go too far" before letting him out to wander freely through the neighborhood, where he'd been run over by a drunk driver who had then crashed into a tree.

"I can't help but think," she sobbed in front of the class. "If I'd just gotten off the phone with my friend and taken Buster for a walk on his leash, he wouldn't have been where he was when that drunk driver ran him over."

Our teacher quickly swept up to the podium and put her arm around the sobbing blur this young woman had become. "Now," the teacher announced, in stern contrast to the person she'd been just minutes a few minutes ago laughing away at my drunken odyssey to Sin City, with the next stop the White House. "We are not to have speeches that glorify driving under the influence or the ingestion of any illegal substances."

She cast a glower in my direction, and I managed to sink deeper into my seat. No matter that without chemical dependency many immortal works of art, ranging from rock and roll songs to paintings to the bodies of countless supermodels, would never have come to pass.

Sitting in that class, back then in the (shudder) year *[4], one had not the right, but the *responsibility* to "just say no."

<u>Thanks,</u> Nancy.[5]

4   Year deleted at insistence of author.

5   Reference to the former First Lady's advice to America during

After three more weeks, I couldn't take the stares of my classmates, even if they weren't even real. As soon as I entered the classroom I imagined everyone was thinking: *Yes, that's him. The one who drinks himself into a stupor and then runs wild, getting behind the wheel and seeking out animals to run over.*

I wound up dropping the class and taking an Incomplete. My Presidential aspirations were on hold, for a semester at least.

The following semester I was dumping my tray into a trash receptacle at one of the commissaries when my elbow bumped against another. I looked and was horrified to find, at my side, that young woman who'd poured her heart out about the cruel death of her dog at the hands of an intoxicated driver.

"I'm sorry," I belted out immediately. "I'm sorry about Buster!"

She stared at me. "Buster?" she asked. "Do I know you?"

"We were in the same class, the public speaking class, where we had to make speeches about stories that changed our lives, and you made a speech about your dog and I made a speech about driving drunk and yelling out to the world that I

---

the beginning of America's disastrous War On Drugs which has succeeded in doing nothing but raising the price of drugs.

was going to try and change it," I blathered.

Her eyes lit up. "Oh yeah!" she piped. "I remember you! You talked about how you and your friends drove to Vegas…"

"Right," I replied. "And you gave that speech about your dog… he was killed by a drunk driver…"

She burst out with laughter. "Oh, *that!* I made that up, um… what was your name again?"

My hand tensed around my tray. I'd spent the past few months waking up from nightmares about me mowing down a variety of canines. "Fuck my name!" I snapped. "What do you mean you *made it up?*"

She smiled nervously. "Chill out, tiger," she tossed her tray on top of the pile. "I knew I wasn't going to be able to top your story, which was *hilarious* by the way."

"Thanks," I nodded numbly.

"Besides," she shrugged. "It seemed like a great opportunity to stretch my acting legs."

"Acting legs." I repeated.

"Well, yeah," she replied. "Do you think Michelle Pfeiffer was *born* a natural actress?"

I'd honestly never given this much thought. But I'd loved her in *Grease 2,* and the song she'd sung, "Cool Rider" was definitely one of my favorite movie songs of all time. As far as this potential starlet before me, I noted her certain resemblance to a character in a long running hour-long drama about the misfortunes of young adults attending college in Southern California. Being that I was a closet fan of the show, I couldn't help but shrug and assure her that she had completely fooled me, she was a wonderful actress, and would she like to come back to my dorm room and have a drink and discuss all this further?

We did, and I found out she actually *did* have a dog growing up. But his name was Hogan, and he'd passed on of natural causes.

Her name was Diana, and like many theater majors, she possessed what I learned in college to term as an "artistic affirmative worldview." In other words, she liked to party and was open to various sexual adventures. We enjoyed ourselves that afternoon, and in keeping with many relationships that blossom in the world of the arts, never saw each other again.

But in a way I knew she would always hold a place in my heart. It was a cursed place, one which flared up periodically and unleashed visions of a pooch being run over by a wild-eyed driver with a half-pint of vodka in one hand and a bullhorn in the other. Even though her story had been a fabricated one, Diana had done a damn good job of delivering it. Some years later she landed a regular spot on a sitcom for a major network. I wasn't surprised. Some people may as well have "STAR" stamped on their foreheads.

Myself, I still dabbled in driving. Until I got my first DUI[6], and after this event I determined I would never drive a car again.

However, at least my Presidential hopes were once again alive and kicking.

❧   ❧   ❧

Being from the Midwest, I get a perverse sensation when I awaken in Los Angeles on a December morning and, instead of contemplating how I'm going to get through the day without having my tongue feel frozen, I simply roll out of bed and launch onto my patio where a warm sun is already greeting the day.

Biking is wonderful here. The weather is mild, and amazingly drivers seem to extend more courtesy to bicyclists than they do to their fellow automobile-wielding combatants of the road. It's as though we bicyclists are granted a pass due to our perceived inability to either afford a car or manage to navigate one.

---

6   No animals, human or otherwise, were harmed in the production of this DUI.

On sunny days it's a true pleasure to bicycle down to the beach, where I'll stare at the waves and try to dredge up meaningful thoughts with pen and paper in hand. Failing this, I'll sip from my from my Gatorade bottle dosed with an ocean of vodka and suddenly the thoughts come free. More writing. More sipping. A few hundred pushups. More sipping. About a hundred pull-ups. More sipping. More watching the waves, a few more immortal thoughts laid down to paper and it's time to call it a day, ride my bike home and watch a rerun of *Malcom In the Middle.*

Yes, life in L.A. can be a slice of paradise. But on this particular day it proved to be paradise interrupted.

Now although I certainly don't advocate driving under the influence, I dare say it's a little different with a bicycle. When you get behind the wheel of a car you're basically getting behind the wheel of a weapon. There are plenty of tales about a drunk driver driving head on into another car, and the occupants of the other vehicle die while he/she miraculously walks away without a scratch. With a bicycle, the odds change a bit. If I were to have a collision with a car, chances are I'd be on the losing end of that confrontation. On the plus side, when intoxicated one tends to fall easier and therefore even wiping out on a bicycle usually doesn't hurt anyone.

So it was with that security in mind that on this day I rode my bike back from the Santa Monica Pier, pumped and buzzed from my workout and the several Vodkarades respectively. At the corner of Fourth Street and Colorado I veered my bike onto the sidewalk. There was no bike lane on this particular street, and automobiles were already piling up in anticipation of rush hour. Moreover there were no pedestrians within sighting distance. Thus there was no danger of me mowing down any mammal, canine or otherwise

Then there came the *scrawk* of a police car behind me.

Why would they be pulling me over? Had I been swerving? It wasn't like I had headlights I'd forgotten to turn on (the *deadest* giveaway that whoever's behind the wheel is most likely blitzed enough to think they can see in the dark). Besides, it was three in the afternoon and the sun was shining.

I pulled my bike over and watched nervously as two officers got out of the car. After all, it *is* possible to get a DUI when on a bicycle. As silly as that may sound, when you have a state as financially bankrupt as California, it starts to make sense given that the fine for said crime is in the thousands of dollars.

One of the officers was a big boned guy who looked bored. The other was an extremely attractive dark-skinned young woman. When I asked them if I'd done anything wrong, she was the one who took the lead.

"It's illegal to ride a bicycle on the sidewalk in Santa Monica." From the grave manner she delivered this bit of information I might as well have asked why it was a crime to possess a hundred thirty-nine ounces of cocaine.

"Ah…" I said. Buzzed as I was, I couldn't help but notice how striking her eyes were. Had we been in a bar I probably would've leaned in closer and tried to think up a sweet nothing to whisper in her ear. But we weren't in a bar, not to mention that while certainly not shit-faced my Blood Alcohol Content was more than likely over the legal limit to be bicycling. So instead of speaking my mind about how the idea of being "guilty" of an infraction such as riding a bicycle on a sidewalk sounded patently ludicrous, I simply said, "I had no idea, Officer."

"Well," she smiled. "Ignorance is no excuse in the eyes of the law."

I nodded. Hell, I'd learned that in one of my high school Criminal Justice classes. While reasonable enough on paper, when one takes a look at some of the laws still on the books in various states, this particular rule of the American Justice system begs one's pause. In Arkansas, for example, men and women can't flirt with one another on a main street. In my home state of Illinois it's considered a crime to urinate in your neighbor's mouth. The only thing more disturbing than the fact that that law's still on the books is that someone felt the need to introduce and pass it.

Now Kentuckians have the right idea, being that they have a law that declares one isn't officially "drunk" unless they "can't hold onto the ground."

Kentucky is a place for me, as is Rhode Island, being they have a law that states any marriage in which either the bride or groom is judged a lunatic or an idiot is considered null and void. Think of how much money people would save if the whole country adopted this law.

However, this wasn't Rhode Island, Kentucky, or any of the other aforementioned states. In California, to the best of my knowledge, marriage between anyone judged an idiot or lunatic is not only permitted but encouraged, and one is free to flirt on a main street, as well as urinate in a neighbor's mouth.

However, apparently riding a bicycle on a Los Angeles County sidewalk is a no-no.

"So if I decide to fight this in court, will I see you there?" I asked her, as she handed me the ticket.

"Absolutely," she replied.

I smiled at the ticket. Her last name rhymed loosely with the word *solvolysis,* which due to way too much free time on my hands I happened to know defined the term used to designate a chemical reaction in which the solute and solvent react to form a new compound. "Nice signature," I nodded.

"Thank you," she snapped her ticket book shut. With authority.

"Then I'll see you in court, officer." I promised.

I walked my bike to the corner, considering myself lucky. Most of the women I've been intimate with during my time in Los Angeles have often remarked how I tend to smell like vodka all the time, even after showering. "Vodka and garlic," is the usual verdict. Here I'd been working out in the California sun and pounding vodka all afternoon; I must've reeked. It was a small miracle these police officers hadn't seen fit to administer a breathalyzer test. So I'd just go to court, pay a fine, and be done with this minor inconvenience.

But as my court date neared, indignation reared its ugly head. Here we were, global warming running wild, tornados and tsunamis being produced by extreme weather patterns, ice caps melting and threatening a real life *Waterworld* (as if the movie wasn't horrifying enough), and all I asked for was to be able to ride my bike openly and freely and live in a room while spending only twenty dollars a month on energy. Now here I'd been ticketed for *bicycling on a sidewalk.* My incomprehension accelerated when I noted that for reasons of her own, this officer who'd given me the ticket had seen fit to specify that I report not to the local Santa Monica or West L.A. Courthouses, but one which was all the way down by Los Angeles International Airport. This meant I would have to awaken at 4:30 in the morning and take three different bus lines in order to make it there by 8:30 A.M.

The days leading up to my trial would start reasonably enough, with me telling myself that if the fine were fifty dollars or under I'd just pay the damn thing. But by the time dusk came, after my cocktail consumption had sufficiently ramped up, I became convinced the judge was going to fine me at least a thousand dollars in order to help prop up California's sagging economy. As I slammed another drink while rocking back and forth in my rocking chair and repeatedly playing Bobby Fuller Four's version of "I Fought the Law," I began to suspect I might receive a sentence of hundreds of hours of community service, or even jail time. By the time I passed out I was ready to not only fight this ticket all the way up to the California Supreme Court but to file a civil lawsuit against the Santa Monica Police Department for unlawful persecution of a man who was just trying to save the planet.

Then a week before my scheduled court date I received a letter from the Santa Monica Police Department, signed by the officer with those prisoner-taking eyes. She was changing the court date from Wednesday to Thursday. I could only assume that this change was due to the fact that she knew I might try and fight this thing, and she wanted to be there for the battle.

The lines, apparently, had been drawn. A battle she wanted, a battle she would get.

I was sober on the Thursday morning I caught the bus down to LAX. Fortunately this didn't last long as I sipped one of my Vodkarades while on the bus. This, combined with the fact I was lightheaded from waking up at 4:30 in the morning, inspired me to conclude that I could either make this date with an unknown destiny into a hassle or an adventure. Though my college degree in Radio, Television, and Film isn't as valuable as, say, a law degree, I had been blessed with some great classes and some great teachers who had introduced me to concepts like existentialism that define destinies as, well, fingers. You can pick which one you're going to raise in relation to the situation you find yourself going through. Some scenarios may call for a middle finger, others a pinky, and most boringly those which demand a finger that's shackled "until death does one part" by a ring.

In this current circumstance, I chose to go the Arthur Fonzarelli route. I looked at my blurred reflection in the bus window as we motored toward LAX, and cocked a thumbs-up that would've made "The Fonz" proud.

Obviously I was already catching a buzz.

Things kept looking up as soon as we arrived at the M.T.A. transit center. I was happy to discover that it was strategically located right next door to the Wild Moose. The Wild Moose is a wonderfully sleazy "Gentlemen's" Club that ranks up there with Gumbo's Clown Room and The GoldMine. Essentially, these establishments are dive bars that happen to feature, along with $3.00 pitchers of watered down beer, topless women dancing and roaming the audience in search of customers who might care for a lap dance. In addition to the $5.00 all-you-can-eat lunch buffet, the other variable that makes these places desirable is dancers whose lack of resemblance to silicone enhanced fashion models is more than made up for by their enthusiasm and willingness to allow a fair amount of groping during a lap dance.

With visions of slightly overweight but energetic strippers writhing in my head, I strolled the half mile to the Courthouse. With any luck I could be done by 11:00 in the morning and be able to hit up the Wild Moose for lunch.

At the Courthouse there was a nervous moment when one of the guards searching us entrants located the three Gatorade bottles in my briefcase. Of course there was no way he could know that these bottles had been "enhanced." Still, the man did give me a curious look.

"You, um, like Gatorade?" he asked.

"Sugar," I explained confidently. "I'm a diabetic, and need to keep the insulin level in my blood locked into proportion with its oxygenized content."

I didn't know what on earth I was talking about. Hell, I didn't know if oxygenized was even a real *word.* (I looked it up later: it is.)

Fortunately the guard obviously didn't know what on earth I was talking about either. He just shrugged, zipped up my bag, and waved me through.

I shared the ride up in the elevator with a police officer who was absent-mindedly tapping the gun strapped to his waist. He began to sniff the air rather deliberately while I held my breath and watched the ascension of the numbered lights. I was going to floor eight. We were at three when he turned to me and stated, "Have you been drinking?"

"Not me," I said, thankful for that theater performance class that had been required for my college major. I flashed back on Mrs. Pushnick's advice: *slant your eye contact so you're staring at the corner of your partner's pupils, keep poise through stillness).*

The officer nodded and went back to fingering his gun. I silently congratulated myself on an adequate performance, but probably the real reason he chose to believe me is that you'd have to be truly stupid/crazy/oblivious to reality to be drinking before nine in the morning in a Los Angeles Superior Court.

I may have been guilty of these charges, but as I got off on the eighth floor of the Courthouse, I was well enough along the way to determine I was definitely *not* guilty of riding my bicycle on a side-walk. I'd been *walking* the damn thing, and there was a very good chance the ticketing officer's wondrous brown eyes had simply misinterpreted what they'd been viewing.

My real father has always stated that if he hadn't become a developer, he would've become an attorney. Though always sup-portive of my crazy career choices, deep down I feel he would've liked to see me become a lawyer. I could imagine his pride were I to call him and inform him of a courtroom victory against a law that deserved to be laughed out of court. If ever such a law existed, it was certainly the one I stood accused of. *Riding a bike on a sidewalk.* Balls, I thought, taking another hit of Vodkarade. The only thing I was guilty of was always wanting to yell, *"Your honor, I object"* in a court-room. Today, I now determined, would be my chance to achieve a lifelong dream. Not only that, but by achieving triumph in this courtroom here today, surely my confidence in my oratory skills would be restored. My Presidential run, which had admittedly been on extended hiatus, could launch back on track.

God Bless you, Your Honor, I pic-tured myself bowing before the judge upon receiving his "Not Guilty" verdict. *And God Bless the United States of America.*

Dangerously buzzed, I strode into that courtroom brimming with confidence. I cast a long deliberate glance around in order to locate my ticketing officer, my future prey who I was going to reduce to a stuttering pile of jelly on the stand.

She was nowhere to be seen.

I stepped up to the bailiff and gave him my name. He leafed through a sheaf of papers as thick as the seventeenth edition of a Biology textbook. "Ah, here we are," he said. "That ticket's been rejected."

I was stunned, and actually more than somewhat disappointed. How could this be? I hadn't yet called a single witness or even gotten the chance to make an opening statement. "Rejected?" I asked. "How?"

The bailiff shrugged. "The officer on record didn't want to pursue it, I guess."

"You *guess?* But I woke up at four-thirty this morning, took three buses here, and now I don't even get my day in court?" I asked.

For the second time that day an officer of the law peered at me as though I were drunk and/or crazy. "Do you *want* a day in court, Mister Michals?"

Uh oh. It occurred to me that with the way I was carrying on I could be arrested and booked on the crime of acting like a fool, an offense which though guilty of many many times, I'd miraculously never been formally charged with.

"No, sir… officer… deputy…" I groped for the proper term, my confidence wilting under the bailiff's steady gaze. Well, it looked like Pops would need to have another kid in order to fulfill his dream of having a lawyer for a son. "I'm sorry," I said to the uniformed officer before me. "I'm not sure what I'm supposed to call you."

"Call me amused for the moment," he snorted. "Now go on home and get some sleep, man."

I nodded and got out of there. Launching out the doors, my ego was already busy turning my semi-meltdown into a victory of sorts. All those visions I'd experienced of a malevolent judge handing down a stiff fine, community service, or thirty days in the hole had been just what I'd somewhat suspected they were: vodka-based rages at imagined injustices.

As a respectable citizen who had somehow escaped the net of the law, I now felt free to enjoy the fabulous view that the eighth floor of the LAX Courthouse offered. Here was a vista that granted a panoramic tour of Los Angeles in one glance. The snow-capped mountains of Big Bear stood in the distance, and palm trees sprouted right beside the buildings of downtown L.A. all the way to the Westside, and the promise of beach, surf, and a setting sun beyond. It wasn't hard to see how this kind of rolling paradise has inspired countless songs and other works of art about just how sweet life can be. I stood, enraptured, on a beautiful So-Cal sun shiny day on this January morning that most likely had the rest of America knee deep in snow. Here was a sprawl of wonder where people who rode bikes were evidently protected by a higher power, its clouds a lining of wise eyelashes that looked down upon a mountainous smile. The wink of the **HOLLYWOOD** sign embedded in the hills provided a cool stare that was hard to turn away from.

I sat on a bench, opened my briefcase, and pulled out my supplies. Pen, paper, iPod, and Vodkarade bottle. In between sentences I observed the comings and goings of various people who had business with the Los Angeles Superior Court. A police officer charged out of one of the rooms and wasn't in the hall ten seconds before he'd called someone and was yelling into his cell about how "some shithead in the D.A.'s office" had "fucked this case in the ass and then made it suck their dick." It occurred to me I could just as soon be sitting at home in my rocking chair watching *The Wire,* but here I was blessed with not only gripping drama but also a much better view of

the Los Angeles skyline, birds chasing
planes as they landed at LAX. Such grace,
both mechanical and animal.

I caught myself growing philosophical,
yet another practice that many might consider a crime in Los Angeles. Yet phi-
losophers do exist out here, lawbreakers
though we may be. Caught in this wild morning I considered that nobody ever seemed
to focus on the gentle descents Los Angeles may bring. Celebrity overdoses, porn
star suicides, child actors either getting
arrested or their own reality shows (or
both); these extreme downfalls offered by
this city were the ones trumpeted to the
world. This was fair, since these *were*
the kind of tales that sold magazines in
grocery store checkout lanes.

But perhaps there was a more graceful
way to sink into L.A., fall into its supposed angels and alleged demons. A middle
ground, maybe? The kind occupied by someone who, though a drunkard, would rather
ride a bike than endanger others by getting behind the wheel of a car. One who
tried to embrace all, regardless of what
religious text they might believe. One
who sometimes had a tad bit of difficulty
differentiating people's sexes. Surely
some would label such a person a sinner
and hate them regardless, but no matter.
From the moment I'd arrived in L.A., I'd
grown into a person I considered both a

non-sinner while at the same time certainly someone worthy of hate.

Above all, as I stared out through a gorgeous view I never would've discovered if it hadn't been for an obscure L.A. law forbidding one to ride a bike on a sidewalk, I could feel nothing but gratitude. Let the Almighties figure it out. I knew I, for the moment, was not only blessed, but was where I belonged.

That could've been the end of this particular story, but two bottles of Vodkarade, several pages of writing, and much music later, I headed back to the M.T.A. Transit Center. It had been a beautiful morning, an illuminating morning, and I was looking forward to the bus ride home and climbing into bed with my stuffed animals.

However, upon arrival at the Transit Center, I was distracted by the Wild Moose. It was *that* kind of strip joint, the kind which opens itself for business at eleven in the morning. Its dank looking doorway and dark bricked structure seemed to be calling my name. Now I don't consider myself the kind of man who would enter a strip joint prior to, well, noon or so, but happily I recalled that when I left the Courthouse its clock had read 11:15.

Lunch, I thought happily. I'll head in for some lunch.

AC/DC's "Highway to Hell" was blasting as I stepped inside. But nobody was onstage. The only people present were the bouncer, two dodgy looking men in checkered coats hogging the lunch buffet, and a fully clothed woman behind the bar, her arms sleeved with tattoos, her face consumed with boredom.

The last time I'd been in the Wild Moose, I'd snorted cocaine off one of the pool tables and gotten amorous with two strippers in one of the back booths. But then, that had been years ago. Before the Great Recession.

This place had, apparently, rolled with the changes.

I was ready to turn back around and head home when I heard, "Well, well, you made it."

I froze. The last time I'd heard that voice it had been promising to see me in court.

I turned and saw Officer *[7], dressed in a bright blue bikini. In the dim light provided by the Wild Moose, her eyes seemed even more blazing.

"What the hell are you doing *here?*" I asked.

She cocked her head a bit and answered quietly, "You seemed a lot more like someone who doesn't ask stupid questions when I first met you."

---

7   Name deleted at insistence of publisher's lawyers.

What was this? Could it be the Santa Monica Police Department was in cahoots with the Wild Moose? Were our taxpayer dollars somehow being funneled to subsidize the existence of strip joints across Los Angeles County? Even though I didn't have any particular *objection* to this, being that money flow is money flow, I thought taxpayers at least had the right to know.

"You're supposed to be a po-"

My ticketing officer cut me off by placing a nicely scented finger against my lips. Then she leaned in and whispered into my ear: "Ssh. Nobody here knows what else I do for a living."

Anyone watching would've thought she was propositioning me for a perfectly legal lap dance. It was a standard scene for a place like this. Even as I cast a glance around, all I saw was the bouncer punching buttons on his Tweeter or Twitter or Twatter or whatever the hell it's called, and the two checkered-coated guys loading up on macaroni and cheese.

Meanwhile, the woman I'd been looking forward to battling in court had taken my arm and was leading me toward one of the rear booths.

"But why…?" I stammered.

"Look, my friend. Times are hard. And this job helps. Plus, we have a ticket quota as officers of the law. We don't have to pursue every ticket, just issue them. So sometimes when I see a guy on a bike on a sidewalk, I give them a ticket and make sure they have to come down here."

My mind was in freefall.

"And how do you know they take the bus…?"

She shrugged. "If they're on bikes, more often than not they don't own a car. So they have to take the bus. Why do you think I made sure you had to report to this L.A. Superior Court instead of the one in Santa Monica?"

It made maddening sense. I marveled at this woman's sheer nerve. Then she pressed herself against me and I began to marvel at other attributes she possessed. I stared fixedly into those eyes that had seduced me and had brought us together. I leaned in closer…

She sputtered laughter, practically spitting in my face.

"What?" I asked.

"You smell more like vodka this morning than you did when I ticketed you," she exclaimed. "You naughty boy, have you been drinking?"

"Wait a minute," I said, hoping to distract her. "If you thought I was drinking that day, why didn't you give me a breathalyzer test?"

She shrugged and smiled. "You seemed like a nice guy. Plus you were on a *bike* for crying out loud. We officers of the law aren't all that rigid, you know."

I assured her, honestly, that I appreciated this fact.

"So how about a dance?" she purred. "Only ten dollars a song. And I promise not to use my handcuffs."

"But handcuffs can be fun," I allowed.

"For those it's twenty a song," she laughed and pushed me down into the booth. I was already justifying this for several reasons. I'd come to the Courthouse with fifty dollars in cash, in anticipation of a fine. Now here was a chance to fulfill a fantasy I'd had roughly since puberty (what red blooded American *hasn't* had a secret desire to be dominated by a policeman/woman in uniform, even though the "uniform" this officer happened to be wearing at the moment was a bikini). I figured the money in my wallet better spent inspiring a beautiful woman to crawl all over me than to justify a stupid law. Briefly I thought back to Diana, the theater major who'd made up that story about her dog getting run over by a drunken driver. It occurred to me I never should have dropped that Public Speaking class; I hadn't really been guilty by association of running down a helpless dog called Buster. As a result I was woefully unprepared to run for President.

But here another woman had let me off the hook for a crime I hadn't really been guilty of, and now I had a new opportunity dancing in front of me. I reached for my wallet as the Clash's remake of "I Fought the Law" began to blast over the Wild Moose's sound system.

I fought the law and the law won...

Five dances later, I emerged from the Wild Moose, reeking of perfume and having paid my "fine."

God Bless Los Angeles. And God Bless the United States of America.

ARE YOU A BOY OR A GIRL?

When I was growing up, my mom had trouble hanging onto female friends. Given her usual mental state, this was no great surprise. She could be gregarious one minute, angry the next. She made friends easily at yoga class or at spiritual seminars, but they rarely lasted beyond the third time an ashtray was thrown at their heads during a discussion about the particular whereabouts of a chakra area.

There was only one woman who stuck it out for years. Mom called her "Mrs. Dunkel." I never heard her refer to Mrs. Dunkel as anything else. From when I was around nine years old I remember Mrs. Dunkel coming over once a month for tea. She wore medium length skirts and matching tops that were usually patterned in stripes. She spoke in a throaty whisper, smoked ultra thin cigarettes, and referred to me as her "little dah-ling." Mrs. Dunkel had a love for old black and white film stars ("the immortals," she called them), spoke often about Greece, and was a member of my mother's Al-Anon meetings.

I adored her, and thought of her as a second mother. But after a few years, I began to notice a slight peculiarity. One afternoon after Mrs. Dunkel had left and we were washing the tea dishes I asked, "Mom, why does Mrs. Dunkel have a beard?"

"It's not a beard," she snapped. "It's what's called a five o'clock shadow. And you'll be getting them soon enough, so don't look down on them."

"Is she in the circus?" I asked hopefully.

"What the hell are you talking about?"

"Is she a bearded lady?" I asked. I'd just read a book about circuses, and had formulated a dream about one day running a circus of my own.

"No, she's not," Mom answered. "Mrs. Dunkel happens to be a man. Now enough with the questions."

Mrs. Dunkel a *man?* This was a bit tough for me to wrap my eleven year old mind around. Why would she want to disguise herself as a woman? Could she be a super secret spy, I wondered excitedly. The only reason I can think of how my mother reconciled her hatred of homosexuals with the fact that Mrs. Dunkel was a man was that Mrs. Dunkel was the only person who had enough strength to stand up to her. Whenever Mom would cock and load an ashtray and start to yell during their afternoon teas, Mrs. Dunkel would simply purr, "Oh, honey puh-leaze." My mom would burst into giggles and look at the ashtray as though it had materialized there magically. She'd then set the ashtray down, having forgotten what she'd been so enraged about in the first place.

I marveled at Mrs. Dunkel's cool under fire, but as I grew older she came around less and less. One afternoon I asked Mom about Mrs. Dunkel, and she replied that Mrs. Dunkel was "back into the abyss."

I didn't know what that meant until almost a year later when I saw Mrs. Dunkel at the grocery store. She was in line, wearing her customary pinstriped combination, but her five o'clock shadow was well approaching midnight. She slurred her words and her arms shook slightly as she paid for her purchases, amongst which I saw were a fifth of Jim Beam and a pack of condoms. I was tempted to say hi, but by this time I was a Freshman in high school and didn't want to risk anyone of any age seeing me talking to someone so obviously different than others.

I never saw Mrs. Dunkel again. However, when I told my mother I was planning to move to Los Angeles immediately after I graduated from high school, her first response was a sarcastic, "Say hi to Mrs. Dunkel's *sisters* for me."

This response I chalked up to her being pissed off that Mrs. Dunkel was now "in the abyss," drinking and having sex, whereas my mom hadn't had a drink or been with a guy roughly since I'd been born.

But then a friend of mine, Jason, also advised me to be on my toes regarding women in L.A.

"Yeah, I know." I said. "But it's not like they can use me for money. I don't have any, remember?"

"Not that," he replied. Then he tapped his throat with deliberation.

"I should clear my throat before talking to them?" I asked.

"The Adam's apple!" he exclaimed. "Make sure they don't have an Adam's apple, because only guys have Adam's apples!"

"Sounds pretty biblical to me," I joked. As entertaining a book as it is, I've never been too good at taking the Bible literally. After all, at one point in the text it recommends that all sons who are drunkards should be stoned to death. "There are plenty of real women in L.A.," I assured Jason. "I'm sure."

"Plenty of drag queens, too. They have a way of making their ass feel like a pussy. Supposedly they give awesome blow jobs." Jason assured me. "And they always have strange names. Like Jacquline or Markita."

"What's so strange about those names?"

Jason looked at me as if I'd just questioned the need to wash one's hands before every meal.

"*Hello!*" he shouted. "They're *guy's* names, like Jack or Mark, but they're…"

He paused, searching for a word. "Elongated," I suggested.

"Right!"

Rather than ask him how it was he seemed to know so much about this, I parried with, "I can tell a guy a mile away. I don't care how much makeup he has on."

Jason slapped my ass and announced with a lisp he just bet I could. I tweaked his nipple and said that he was damn right I could. Amazingly, the afternoon ended without one of us blowing the other.

Jason wasn't alone. My other friends all assured me that Los Angeles was full not only of homos but of men dressed up as women who would seduce me with the best blowjobs I'd ever had.

My first few years in L.A., I did meet a few women who were definitely suspect. Though they were a hell of a lot better looking than Mrs. Dunkel, there were still giveaways: falsies used to make them appear to have firm breasts beneath their skintight tops (one confided into me that she never left home without her "nipple shields.") Also, I learned that if one is talking to a woman for more than ten minutes and the woman still hasn't raised her voice above a whisper, chances are there's a reason.

Though I'd been fairly inebriated on the occasions I met these various drag queens, I was successfully able to spot them and politely resist their advances. Still, I was curious about the world in which they inhabited. The only places I'd encountered them were dance clubs, a small very dark bar in Santa Monica ominously known throughout various circles as The Dungeon, and Hubert Selby Jr.'s book *Last Exit to Brooklyn.*

I often wondered how these conquerors of both sexual poles occupied their daylight hours. Did they go to their day jobs in drag? Did they *have* day jobs? Were they all strippers or drag queens of the night? Was there an international trust fund for drag queens? And why did they always seem so happy?

Despite my curiosity, I didn't want to know too much. Selby's *Last Exit to Brooklyn* had taught me that to get mixed up with a drag queen could leave one a confused sobbing mess.

But when one lives and drinks in L.A., one does tend to get lured into situations of compromised inhibitions, if not outright experimentation. The particular adventure of which I speak started innocently enough when my friend Patty invited me to a Christmas party being given by a hospital situated in the San Fernando Valley, one she had worked for in the past. She'd quit long ago but still maintained a relationship of sorts with one of the head administrators. The hospital was renting out a restaurant. Catered food, open bar, and what Patty referred to as "live entertainment."

The party began with an abundant display of food. Roasted lamb, grilled sea bass, filet mignon and teriyaki flavored tofu burgers. Patty, who wasn't working at the time, was grabbing entrees with both hands. No sooner would a steaming plate of crab ravioli be placed at the table when it would be gone.

"Where are you putting all this?" I asked her, as politely as possible. Despite being unemployed, Patty managed to eat well and was a Big Beautiful Woman around two hundred and fifty pounds.

"In here!" she whispered with a smile, and held up her purse, which was roughly the size of a small wastebasket. "These holiday parties are great places to stock up on food. Whatever isn't eaten is just going to be thrown away anyway."

Logical enough for me. I stood in front of Patty and provided her with cover as she continued to load up her purse. Then I decided to stock up myself and made my way over to the bar. They were serving top shelf vodka, and I was impressed that the bartenders wouldn't allow me to tip them. "We're being taken care of," they told me. Feeling proud to be at such a classy affair, I celebrated by ordering a double Grey Goose and Cranberry.

Then came the live entertainment. Taking the stage was a stripper who introduced herself as Xixa ("Zee-zaa," she pronounced with a wink and a roll of her tongue over her teeth). Her taut body was accentuated by a black bra and thigh-highs. Perfectly pouted lips, olive skin and a rear end that looked solid enough to hold up a piano. Her stiletto heels were potential murder weapons.

Madonna's "Vogue" erupted and Xixa began to dance. Standing at the bar, top-shelf vodka swirling inside of me, I felt emboldened enough to wink at her.

Damned if she didn't wink back.

Granted, it's a stripper's job to flirt just suggestively enough with the clientele in order to bring in more tips. However, Xixa wasn't making any forays into the audience seeking dollar bills. Therefore I assumed she, like the bartender, was not allowed to even accept tips. I had another swallow of my second double vodka and furthermore assumed that this meant she must've winked back at me because she actually *liked* me.

When Xixa whipped out a crucifix from her leather purse and rubbed it against her crotch, my fellow partygoers, most of who (Patty had informed me earlier) were doctors or in some way part of the hospital administration, went wild.

"Get it wet!" a portly man to my right shouted.

"Show them how it's done!" a woman at the end of the bar, clad in a red sequined dress, hooted.

I made a mental note to never allow myself to be admitted to this particular hospital, under any circumstances.

"Now who wants to dance?" Xixa challenged, in the proper tone of a dominatrix looking for someone buzzed and with enough lack of self-respect to participate in some kind of naughty, and most probably humiliating, debauchery in front of hundreds of hungry eyes.

Her gaze met mine. *Uh-oh.*

I held out my drink and waved it back and forth as though trying to ward off an oncoming car, but she seemed to interpret this as a semi-salute, because she grabbed my wrist and pulled me onto the dance floor.

Having no idea what was expected of me, I did what came naturally. I slammed the remainder of my drink and began to rip my shirt off. But evidently Xixa had other plans for me. She quickly spun me around and thrust me chest first into a folding chair. I sat there, dazed, wondering drunkenly if this was part of some grand scheme, when I felt the unmistakable smack of an object against my buttocks.

I looked back and saw Xixa brandishing the very same crucifix she'd been rubbing between her legs only a minute ago.

"My sweet darling," she whispered, her strawberry tinted breath swarming my ear. "Are you a bad boy?"

I tried to conjure up an appropriate response, something along the lines of, "Well, I'm being spanked by a leather clad stripper on a stage in front of a bunch of strangers. I don't suppose I'm exactly a *good* boy."

But words failed me. I was too caught up in remembrance of the first time I'd been spanked with a crucifix. When I'd been around twelve years old, I'd awoken and discovered I was sleeping above a foreign, sweet smelling stain. As I'd been frantically trying to peel the sheets off my bed with a vague idea of burning them and destroying the evidence my mom, who had evidently been pacing the hallway in one of her manic states, had burst into my room and caught me in the act. Upon seeing the stained sheets she'd determined a spanking was necessary. The handiest object had been the crucifix hanging on the wall above my bedpost. Though technically my family was Jewish, with my grandfather having converted to Judaism in order to be able to marry my Jewish grandmother, Mom had always insisted upon hanging a crucifix above my bed "just in case He arose."

The Lord may not have risen that night but something else sure had, and then done considerably more. And as a result, a spanking had come.

Though religious symbols had long since lost a great deal, though not all, meaning to me, this time with Xixa brandishing the cross was considerably more enjoyable than with my mother, if only because I wasn't lying in a puddle of my own discharge.

After ten good whacks, Xixa blew me a kiss and pushed me back into the mass of onlookers. I accepted congratulations from some people in the crowd and went back to the bar as Xixa began to deep throat her crucifix to the opening strains of Madonna's "Like a Prayer."

At the bar, the woman in the red dress who'd urged Xixa to "show them how it was done" complimented me on my willingness to take a spanking. Intrigued, I began talking to her. Still my attention kept wandering back to the dance floor, where Xixa was now spraying herself down with oil to Madonna's "Ray of Light."

After I'd looked away from the red dressed woman for the fourth time, the next time my eyes drifted back her way she was gone.

Such is life. I ordered another top-shelf drink and turned back to the dance floor only to see Xixa betraying me. She'd picked another random guy from the crowd and was spraying him with whip cream while at the same time hosing him down with a water bottle shaped like a dildo.

How fickle she was, I thought. But then the vodka reminded me that she was just doing her job. She'd *meant* it with me.

Xixa finished off her act by dry humping a fire extinguisher to the timeless rhythm of 2 Live Crew's "Somebody Say Hey (We Want Some Pussy.)" She left the dance floor to wild applause. I tried to track her but lost her in the crowd.

Gradually the party thinned out. Patty came rushing up to me at the bar. "I need you," she said. "I need you now!"

"Yes, my dear." I replied. Drunk as I was, I embraced all two hundred and something pounds of her and was ready to French kiss her when she pushed me off.

"What are you doing?" she demanded.

I had no clue. "You said you needed me," I said.

"Not for that, you idiot. Richard, my friend who invited me here, is shaking everyone's hand as they leave the party. There's no way I can carry my purse out with so much food stuffed in it without looking suspicious. So I stashed it in the ladies bathroom. There's a back door near the bathrooms. Your mission, should you choose to accept it, and I *know you will,* being that I've brought you to this great party with all this free vodka, is to go into the ladies room, get my purse, then head out the back. I'll be there waiting for you."

"But won't Richard get suspicious if he doesn't see me leaving with you?" I asked.

"No, he doesn't even know who you are. Nobody here does."

She had a point. Secure in my anonymity, I had one more cocktail ("triple, please") while watching the partygoers disperse. After ten minutes, the allotted time Patty had told me it would take her to get around back, I looked around for the rear hallway. Nowhere to be found.

I asked the bartender directions to the ladies room. Without missing a beat, he pointed out the rear hallway I'd missed. I wasn't sure, but I think he wagged his finger at me.

I stepped with exaggerated purposefulness (read: drunkenly) into the hall, and after a cursory look around, I entered the women's washroom.

At first it seemed deserted. But then I glanced to my left and saw a wild eyed creature, temples pulsing, lipstick smear on their flushed cheek, and a sinister grin fit for a drunken predator-

Jesus. It was me.

"Do what you came here to do and get out," I said to my reflection. I looked around, eyes scanning over the urinals, the stalls, and finally landing on the wastebasket Patty had described.

A stall door opened. Out came Xixa. She'd changed from her black lace and garters into a short jean skirt and a purple t-shirt with pink lettering that read: "IF YOU'RE GONNA TOUCH IT, YOU MIGHT AS WELL…"

"Hello there," she said.

My first time being caught in a women's restroom. How to explain it? I chose not to. "I don't usually do this," I explained.

"Really?" Xixa purred. "What do you usually do?"

"I'm here to get something," I said quickly, trying not to feel like a stalker as I made my way over to the wastebasket.

Xixa eyed me curiously as I pawed through the assorted paper towels, tissues, and condom wrappers piled in the wastebasket. No purse full of food. Someone had evidently stolen Patty's food rations for the next three weeks.

I looked up and noticed Xixa had taken a few steps my way. "Sorry," I said. "I didn't find what I was looking for."

"Are you sure about that?" Xixa gave a slight pout, which I've always been a sucker for. Next thing I knew I was kissing her neck, and this led to my nibbling on her neck.

"Follow me," she whispered into my ear.

It only took about ten seconds for Xixa to deftly guide me into a stall, unbuckle my belt and pull down my pants. She was a speedy gal. Then she had my penis in her hand while murmuring about how quickly I was growing. Within seconds she was kneeling down and fulfilling the promise she wore on her t-shirt. Her skill combined with the facts that we barely knew one another and were in a public restroom came together to make this one of the most wickedly orgasmic experiences of my life.

Many people, when confronted with either extreme horror or extreme pleasure, call out to God for something… assistance… explanation… the hope that there's some possible meaning to life. Suffice to say while in that toilet stall with Xixa my cries to God were those solely of pleasure and gratitude. As I came I thought, as I usually do when orgasming, that perhaps there was that elusive pot of gold at the end of the old rainbow.

She stood up and kissed me. "You're awesome, Xixa." I told her.

She chuckled. "Xixa's my stage name. But here's my card. My real name, and my real number." I immediately pocketed the glossy business card she slipped into my hand. "Thanks." I said, then remembered Patty waiting out back. "I gotta go."

"Then go, silly," she blew me a kiss.

I hurried out of the stall and looked at myself in the mirror. I smiled casually, trying to exude the image of a rock star who'd just had a beautiful stripper suck his dick within minutes of meeting her. Even my own semen in my mouth from when she'd kissed me a moment ago tasted good, almost like vodka.

I floated out of the restroom and sailed down the hallway, then through the rear of the building. Patty was waiting in her car.

"Where's my purse?" she asked.

"Somebody must've taken it," I said. "I looked in the wastebasket, just like you said, and it wasn't there."

"Damn!"

I offered to spring for burgers from Jack In the Box on the way home and this seemed to calm her. As we drove along I basked in the glow of a great night. Free cocktails, an awesome blowjob, and the phone number of a beautiful woman.

"Where'd you disappear to during Xixa's act?" I asked Patty. "She was pretty hot, you know."

Patty snorted. "You mean *he* was pretty hot."

There are little details in life that are deceptively easy to miss. The color of someone's eyes, a positioning of an axe at a murder scene, or, in this case the fact that next to the wastebasket I'd searched for Patty's stash of food in had been a row of urinals. Men's urinals.

"He?" I asked quietly.

"Richard told me he was going to hire a drag queen to shake the party up. I went out to smoke a cigarette during his act. I heard he got some suckers up there to spank and whatnot."

"Yeah," I said in a carefully controlled monotone. "They were really into it."

"Well, this is L.A." Patty concluded. "A lot of freaks in this town."

All sorts of realities began crashing down on me. I wasn't a rock star. A beautiful woman had never just pulled me into a bathroom stall and given me a blowjob. My semen didn't actually taste *that* much like vodka.

"... surprised someone would have the nerve to do that." Patty was saying.

"Do what?" I asked. Voluntarily get spanked with a crucifix while others looked on? Mistakenly sneak into the men's restroom instead of the ladies? Get blown by a drag queen in a toilet stall? My life, I realized, was filled with incidents that required either abundant nerve or abundant stupidity. After several tense moments debating between the two, I settled on abundant recklessness.

"Steal food from a wastebasket," Patty said, answering my *do what.*

"Like you said," I sighed. "A lot of freaks in this town."

Three Jumbo Jack burgers later (two for her, one for me), Patty dropped me off at my building. I went into my apartment and poured a cocktail. I drank that and poured another, figuring I might need it. I pulled out the business card Xixa had pressed into my hand. She was clad in a tank top and bikini bottoms, straddling a Harley Davidson and gazing out at the world like there was nothing more she would rather do than give it the best blowjob it ever had.

Then I poured a third and after a few swallows got up the nerve to look closer. This was undeniably a beautiful individual. If Xixa was in fact a guy, I told myself firmly, at least she was a *hot* guy. Then the lettering at the bottom of the card caught my eye.

Shawna XOXO (310) 555-9374

My friend Jason's admonition came back to me. *Hello! They're guy's names, like Jack or Mark, but they're…*

"Elongated," I said to myself.

I retrieved *Last Exit to Brooklyn* from my bookcase, read a few pages, toasted my doppelganger with another cocktail, then lay down and laughed myself to sleep.

A confused mess, yes. But at least I was a laughing one.

NOTES FROM A BIZARRE AND LIFE-THREATENING VISIT TO SPAIN

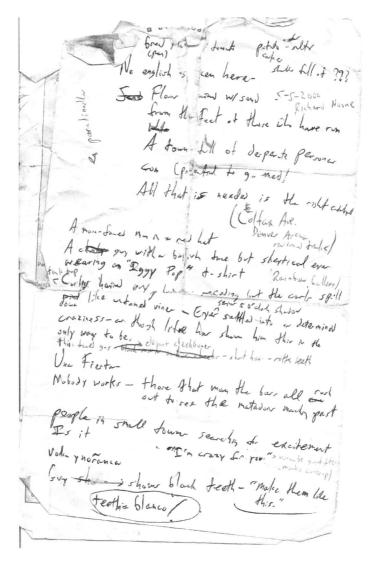

...tictan barbari
slippery w/ sand.
Scene of grass,
they fuck war guy in
Spain.

Someone dills oversteway
like amputee
In España, ~~they~~ elise
some people like lawyer,
some see them as meat?
joker!

In Spain, they've never
heard of lung cancer,
Or emphysema—even though ½

youth is dispersed

you never see million dollar money
by from dudes as mothers who
in the world for me (esp. France)

(& then probably
have it)
guy walks 64 w/ bandages — left thigh (both ears pierced)
on his leg (tattoo of an → guy molden man, black sunk he, tall oth blue
angel on his back) short
susy)
they get a bad of pain jew

Some of them (precious) have money teeth.

Say: "España es bonita" — He looked at me like "fuck
(This is a shithole, dusty pueblo — graffiti everywhere (you,
older people tuck in their shirts tourist."
~~just~~ let them hang

? Heaven + Hell exist in diffet <u>languages</u>?

The preceding pages certainly require an explanation of sorts. To the best of my knowledge they are the result of a backpacking trip Shawn took to Spain, one that almost, according to his version, cost him his life.

Though Shawn was known to exaggerate on occasion, for some reason I believe the story he told me one afternoon in a locker room, somewhere in Arizona, while we were getting ready for a match that night. Maybe because he seemed so reluctant to share it, as if this particular experience in his life was one precious enough to make him uncomfortable revealing it to others. Or it might've been how wistful he seemed while telling the tale, as if this were a story not only of travel across the globe, but within himself, to a place he might never find again. Whatever possessed him to tell me I never discovered.

Apparently he'd gone on a "Spanish sojourn" for the reason many aspiring writers do. Hooked on the Hemingway myth, he thought that simply running with the bulls and drinking himself into stupors would transform him into a brilliant writer. Unfortunately he arrived a week too late for Pamplona's annual celebration. So he hunted down a Corrida de toros *in a remote pueblo by the name of Iscar. "This village is so remote," he*

related with a hint of pride as he jabbed
a small blade across the top of his right
eyebrow so he'd be able to bleed easier
in the match we were set to have that
night. "You won't even find it on a map."

Shawn went on to tell me about that
fateful day, which began when he took a
morning bus from the city of Valladolid,
where he'd been staying at a hostel. He
took his luggage with him, planning to
spend a few days "roughing it" in a town
no one in the hostel had ever heard of. It
was almost a hundred miles south before
the bus turned off the main highway onto
a dirt road. Twenty minutes later the bus
rumbled into the village of Iscar and
abruptly stopped at a corner amidst rows
of squat dwellings that looked as if they
could be toppled by a strong wind.

By that time Shawn was the lone pas-
senger on the bus, and he'd gotten up and
asked the bus driver, in seriously broken
Spanish, when they would reach the bus
depot. The bus driver laughed heartily
and replied, Cerrado. Es Fiesta!

Shawn got off the bus and looked around.
The streets were littered with plastic
cups and beer bottles. When he asked the
bus driver for directions to the nearest
hostel, all he got back was a shrug.

In the background there were shouts
that clashed with screams. Surrounded by
low structures that he described as look-

*ing as though they'd been dragged from
the sea and left to dry and eventually
crumble in the heart of Spain, Shawn began
to feel nervous. This was certainly not a
tourist destination.*

"*It was the kind of town Clint Eastwood used to find himself drifting into in
all those Spaghetti Western classics,*"
*was how Shawn put it, as he made sure the
tie to his spandex tights was tucked to
the left.* "*And I didn't know much Spanish, but I sure as hell knew I wasn't as
tall as Clint Eastwood.*"

*Though determined to continue on with
his adventure Shawn did acknowledge that
caution might be the better part of valor,
and thus asked the bus driver what time
the next bus left.*

"Tres y media," *the bus driver said.*
"Despues de eso, nada. Manana."

*Shawn checked his watch. Almost noon.
Three and a half hours to find shelter,
a bull to run with, and a cocktail. Not
necessarily in that order.*

*With the bus depot closed, there was
no immediate place Shawn could stash
his luggage. So he wheeled his suitcase
through a maze of side streets devoid of
markers of any kind. Grit crackled under
his feet. Once Shawn reached the main
avenue, a group of men and women shouted
to him from a sidewalk bar:* "Italiano!
Italiano!"

Relieved, Shawn assumed he'd found a group of fellow tourists and hurried over. Within seconds it became apparent these were locales. When he asked them 'que hora es corrida de toros,' they responded, 'desmiado tarde.'

"I'd missed the damn thing," Shawn told me as he pulled up his kneepads, the words BORN and TO sprayed on them respectively. "Again. So I figured I might as well at least get drunk and get to know some of the local town folk. When they asked me where I was from, I thought I'd be slick and tell them Canada. Friends had warned me that in small Spanish pueblos, being from America isn't always a good thing. It didn't matter. As soon as I said 'Canada,' they got a weird gleam in their eyes and drawled 'Norteamericano.'"

But being as he'd already been poured a drink and given a cigarette, Shawn didn't want to leave too abruptly and have them think him rude. He was even about to buy a fresh round for the table and was reaching into his pocket for some cash when one of the only two women at the table kicked him lightly on his shin. "Don't," she mouthed at him. "Don't take your money out here."

Though Shawn told himself that she was probably just having a laugh at his expense, the first sparks of alarm that he *may have wandered into a situation that could land him in a foreign jail in the middle of nowhere began to make themselves known.*

Shawn tried speaking to the men he was sharing a table with, but his Spanish was, as he put it, challenged. At one point he said to the man on his left, who was wearing an Iggy Pop t-shirt and had a thick shaggy moustache, that Espana es muy bonita.

"The guy looked at me, and it was all there in his eyes." Shawn shook his head, lacing up his boots. "Fuck you, tourist."

At this point those sparks of alarm Shawn had been feeling began to flare. They were quickly ushered into an inferno when the man at the head of the table, with sun burnt skin and long hair that flared in all directions, head-butted his beer bottle. Pieces of glass and streams of beer flew.

The other men began to point at this individual and whisper to Shawn that when this guy drank, he became "muy loco."

"That was one of the bits of Spanish I was pretty familiar with," Shawn grinned as he wound neon green tape around his wrists. "Next thing I know this guy's gotten up and is coming my way. He's got wild looking eyes; his pupils looked ready to pop out of their sockets. There were thin trails of blood and beer

dripping down his cheeks. Looked like a
Spanish Terry Funk[8]. He places a hand on
my shoulder. His flesh smelled like beer,
pork, and beans. He leers at me and asks,
'Americano?' So I used one of the only
other Spanish phrases I'd memorized and
replied, 'Yo soy escritor.'"

"What's that mean?" I asked Shawn.

He paused in the midst of smearing his
bare chest with baby oil and shook his
head as though I'd just asked where babies
came from. "It means, 'I am a writer,'"
he said, then shrugged. "I mean up 'till
that point I really hadn't written much,
but I knew I'd always kind of wanted to
be one. And it seemed like a good thing
to say at the time."

"So what happened?"

Shawn's new friend had apparently begun
to laugh, then leaned in close and smiled
widely. Shawn described his breath as a
combination of cat shit and wet newspaper.
The view wasn't much better either. Rot-
ting teeth, though the guy couldn't have
been much older than his mid-twenties.

According to Shawn, the guy murmured
in perfect English, "I'm crazy for you."

By now the other men at the table were
in hysterics. Shawn was laughing too, very
nervously. Was this all a joke? He looked

---

8   One of the greatest, wildest, and all-around craziest professional wrestlers. Ever.

to the woman who'd warned him against taking out his money, and found her gone. He was alone in a village where locals were already getting hammered at two in the afternoon. Being someone who prided himself on knowing a thing or two about alcohol consumption, Shawn was well aware that quite a few people who are jolly at two in the afternoon sometimes turn fairly angry by eight o'clock at night.

"So I took a big gulp of beer," Shawn said, as he took a moderate sip from his Diet Mountain Dew bottle. "And I checked my watch as casually as possible. It was a quarter past two. So I had an hour and fifteen minutes to extricate myself from the situation and catch the last bus out of town before the sun went down."

I was caught up enough in his story to not bother asking what extricate meant. I just assumed it meant, "get the hell out of Dodge."

"So I did a lot of smiling," Shawn smiled as he capped the Diet Mountain Dew bottle, "Along with plenty of nodding, and an abundance of looking back over my shoulder to make sure I wasn't being followed as I made my way back down the dusty streets, none of which had a street sign."

"Wow," I concluded. "Sounds like a hell of a time."

"Yeah, but it was more than that," Shawn shrugged on the white fringe leather jacket he wore to the ring. "After I caught the bus back and arrived in Valladolid, I checked into a hotel, because I just wasn't in the mood for another night in a hostel. Besides, I guess in some strange way I felt the day I'd just been through had entitled me to a warm bath and clean sheets instead of being kept awake by the sounds of mice scrounging through empty potato-chip bags along with the snores of seven other fellow travelers."

I nodded, trying to imply that I sympathized. The furthest, or farthest, I'd been out of the United States was swimming in the Pacific Ocean off of Malibu.

"So that night in the bathtub I sipped from a bottle of vodka I'd bought, you know, to calm my nerves." Shawn said slowly, as he applied black lipstick to accentuate his Goth Rocker gimmick. "But then I began to think. Here I'd just gone through this wild experience, one in which I'd declared myself a writer. Hell, it was when I said I was a writer that that crazy guy had started laughing and left me alone. For all I knew, me saying I was a writer had saved my life. But the thing was, I hadn't written a damn thing. So I got out of the tub and trooped my naked ass into the *hotel room and grabbed a piece of paper and a pen. Then I went back into the tub and just wrote and wrote about the day, about the trip… about the people I'd met and the situations I'd observed… I was making notes because I didn't want to forget these times, and I guess I thought down the road I could use them as a basis for some kind of opera, like a demented* Les Miserables *or something like that. Even though I knew nobody would probably ever read them, I still enjoyed the act. I finished off the bottle of vodka and filled up two pages with notes. It was…"*

Shawn paused and put down his lipstick container. Pursed his lips. "It was an experience," he continued. "A playwright, John Guare, once wrote about the problem human beings have in keeping experiences special. That night was the night I realized that the way I could keep experiences special was to write about them."

Shawn stood. "It was one of the happiest nights of my life."

I must've been giving him an odd look because he suddenly seemed agitated. He jerked on the wraparound sunglasses he always wore to the ring. "What?" he snapped, his eyes concealed behind mirrored frames.

"So did you ever write about your trip?" I asked. "The demented opera?"

Shawn shook his head slowly. "Nah," he replied, as though embarrassed. "All I have for now are those notes I scribbled down in that bathtub. Maybe someday..."

He flashed a smile as quick as a match's strike. "After I'm crippled at age thirty-four from being a pro wrestler for so many years." He shot a playful but precise jab that stopped just short of my jaw. "Speaking of which, we still have to work out a finish for our match."

I can't even recall which one of us ended up winning our bout that night. But I'll always remember the way Shawn related his story, and how later on he told me he wanted to return to Iscar one day, when he'd done more work on learning the traditions and the language of the land, when he'd have no fear of being imprisoned and be able to run as furiously as any bulls he might encounter.

I've no idea if he ever made it back there. When I found the aforementioned notes in his apartment, I was tempted to destroy them. They were personal, disjointed, not making much sense, scribbled while naked, drunk, and alone in a bathtub. But Shawn Michals had an impact on my life, and that's one of the reasons I'm publishing some of his work.

He may see all this as an invasion of his privacy. He may hate me for it, he may love me for it.

In this case, I suppose I made the decision to follow his example; share a story, keep it as a treasured experience, and take my chances.

- B.P.

NO CAR, NO CELLPHONE, NO PROBLEM

When I tell people in Los Angeles I don't have a car, the most consistent response is "Who the hell lives in Los Angeles without a car? What are you, Shawn? Some kind of psycho?"

Nolo contendere, baby. But damned if I'm going to admit this. Though I do my best to plead innocence, people still react as if I've told them I don't have a functioning pair of lungs. (L.A. air being what it is, it is entirely possible that one of my lungs has called it quits).

I express a desire to not leave a carbon footprint, and a general love for ice caps, stable seasons, and those cute looking polar bears that would no doubt give me a big hug for not taking away their habitat instead of eating me at the drop of a hat.

The truth, as is the case with most truths, is not quite as noble. My dalliance with driving in L.A. ended just six months after I arrived. There was a slight misunderstanding between me and the Department of Motor Vehicles, with me misunderstanding that I was sober enough to drive. Alas, with a BAC of .20, I was not.

The police officers who pulled me over were both pleasant sorts. I'm sure I made things easier, both on myself and them, when after staggering through the "walk the line" test, I simply turned around and clasped my hands behind my back.

"You're a good guy," I heard one of the officers say, as he put the cuffs on me.

Instead of impounding my car, one of them drove it to a side street and parked it. I was thankful for this, being that it saved me not only a three hundred dollar impound fee, but also the need to find a new place to live. I was also thankful they didn't check the backseat. Among a sea of fast food wrappers and Racing Forms, there were vials of the steroid Deca-Durabolin, syringes, and at least three empty pint bottles of vodka I hadn't gotten around to dropping in a recycling bin.

At the station, I shook the hands of my arresting officers, both of whom wished me luck, as they put it, "in my new home."

Now I can see people wishing you luck when you're buying a lotto ticket or attempting to break a world's record of some kind. But being wished luck before entering a jail cell is downright disconcerting.

My new home turned out to be a cell with twenty bunks to a row on either side.

I walked down the rows, making as little eye contact as possible as I scanned the Hispanic and African-American faces checking me out. *You are not afraid,* I repeated silently to myself, hoping there was at least *one* other token white guy in here.

I found him at the last bunk on the right. I hopped on the bed above his. I thought of what my mother had said to me just a year ago, when I'd announced I was heading to L.A. as soon as I graduated high school so I could get as far away from her as possible.

"You're gonna be a drunken shitstain just like practically every goddamn male in your father's family. You won't be out there six months and you're gonna be in jail, and probably taking it up the ass." She stared at me with a suspicious eye. "And probably liking it, you goddamn latent queer!"

Here I was, six months into L.A, and I was living up to Mom's timeline as far as being in jail went.

But as far as taking it up the ass, latent queer or not, I certainly didn't want my first homosexual experience to take place in a jail cell. Thus I didn't sleep that night, keeping a vigilant eye out for potential rapists. The only way to tell passage of time was a light bulb outside the cell. I spent who knows how

long gripping the sides of my thin plastic mattress and keeping my ass sealed
securely to its surface. Finally the
light bulb that served as an artificial
sun outside our cell began to brighten as
a signal of the oncoming morning. About
this time I heard screams coming from
beyond the rear wall. A large steel door
was embedded in the wall, but there was a
thin space beneath the door and the concrete ground. I hopped down and peered
into the crack.

The other side of the wall turned out
to be the ladies' cell. I saw two women
holding another in a compromising position. Another woman was spanking the victim, a Hispanic in a short skirt.

"Check this out!" I whispered to my
bunkmate. He did. Soon half our cell was
back there, taking turns watching the drama
unfold on the other side of the steel.

"Spank that naughty ass, girl!" one of
my cellmates called out.

There was a pause in the action on the
other side. Then a high pitched retort:
"Get outa here you lil' punk! You wanna
see this shit, slide some money over!"

"I got *ten inches* to slide over!"

All of us male prisoners chuckled away
at this, while on the other side the
women resumed spanking their victim.

That broke the ice, and my cellmates
and I wound up spending the morning roll-

ing cigarettes and passing them around. It turned out my suspicions about someone raping me had been unnecessary. Most of my fellow inmates were gang members, true. Felons as well. But nobody was in there on a murder rap or anything, and they were mostly just bored, eager to ride out this latest stay in jail. As we passed cigarettes back and forth, I grew more and more comfortable. The bunks weren't bad actually. They made fine seats, and actually fostered a kind of comradeship, an "all for one and one for all" attitude. An enterprising person, I reasoned, could fill an L.A. downtown loft with bunks, black out all windows, hang dimmer lights throughout the space and promote it as a hip club called "JAIL."

Strange brilliant things such as this can happen in L.A. In this mass of palm trees and sand, scared runaways from home have grown into worldwide symbols of unbridled confidence oozing with sexuality. "Degenerates that will never amount to anything" learn how to play music, or tell jokes, or just be themselves and become millionaires who entertain millions with their specific artistic gift. Hell, in Los Angeles it's possible for a former bodybuilder turned actor to become the Governor of California using a slogan he uttered in movies in which he played a killer robot.

Certainly "The Guv-o-nator" wouldn't have been intimidated had he been in my current situation. I tried to follow his example and assumed a confident air. One of my cellmates, Red, was a Latino who had a scar that wound all the way around his face. It was as if a snake laced with acid had given him a hug. He'd just regaled us with his tales of working in a morgue, and how one of his favorite pastimes was to "get stoned with the corpses and just chill," when I asked him, "How'd you get that scar, holmes?"

He leveled me with a cool stare. "What the fuck do you care, white meat?"

Oh shit. I'd broken taboo, a rule of some kind. Was it because I'd used the term *holmes* when I actually didn't even have a clear idea of what it was supposed to designate?[9] Because I was getting a kinky thrill out of being in jail, knowing I would probably be out soon on my own recognizance, while most of these people around me had already referred to the cell as "second home sweet second home?"

Regardless, I had to answer him. "Just curious," I said. Whispered, actually,

---

9   I was later to learn that the use of *Holmes* dates back to when Larry Holmes defended his WBC title against Gerry Cooney. Though the champion, Holmes was considered the underdog. He was black, Cooney was white. After a wild match from which Holmes emerged victorious, he and Cooney became friends. Holmes has been integrated into American slang to indicate all underdogs, scrappers, fighters, etc.

because I was too scared to raise my voice at all. As I held his gaze, I thanked the Gods for my first semester of theater class, as well as for watching endless hours of professional wrestlers staring into a camera and looking like there was nothing more they'd like to do than rip someone's head off.

Suddenly my challenger burst out laughing. "Just kidding, gringo," he drawled. Then he asked what I was in for.

I had a feeling that a DUI charge wouldn't be dastardly enough to cut it with this fellow, so I launched into a fictionally revolutionized account of what had brought me to jail, laying it down about how I ran a steroid smuggling ring based out of Tijuana. In the past couple months I had actually smuggled steroids back from Tijuana, and had sold some (though only enough to pay for my own steroid use). I was certainly big enough, at the time, to make my story seem halfway believable. But when I got to the part of my having put one of the cops that arrested me in the hospital, my cellmates burst into laughter.

"Brotha, this cell is for parole violators and DUIs only."

Sheepishly I admitted that I actually was in for a DUI. But, I lied emphatically, I *had* mouthed off to the cops as they brought me in.

Red, Crunch, Dread, Sammy… all my new friends began warning me about something called "County," which was L.A. County Jail. I knew about the place. My images of it had been shaped by television and movies. Race riots, tuberculosis in the air, rats scampering over you as you slept. To actually comprehend that I might wind up there effectively destroyed what was left of my .20 BAC buzz.

Don't, my new comrades advised me, ever let anyone get you stoned in County. "They'll wait until you're all screwed up, bra." Dread nodded knowingly. "Then gang your ass."

At that time, though not up to defining the term *holmes,* I could pretty much connect the dots on *gang your ass.*

"Shut up, bitch," I whispered to Mom's warning that once I got to Los Angeles I'd be taking it up the ass and liking it.

"Whazzat?" Dread said to me, his eyes boring into mine.

"Sounds…" I gasped. "Sounds like a bitch."

Thankfully Dread was distracted by Sammy, who clapped Dread on the shoulder and chuckled about how many nights he'd been in County, nestled in his cot minding his own business and drifting off to sleep, when he would suddenly hear the screams of some poor inmate getting raped in a cell somewhere on the block. Dread nodded along wistfully, the way I one day hoped to reminisce with someone about being kept awake by the gentle sound of ocean waves outside a penthouse suite at some beachfront resort.

The bulb outside our cell kept getting brighter throughout the day, and I began to wonder if I'd be in there for another night. But then as the bulb started to dim, a bailiff came by and called out, "Michals, Shawn. You're out."

I nodded farewell to the people I'd spent the last twelve hours with. As I walked toward the exit, I heard Red call out, "Hey, Michals, Shawn."

I turned back. He was running his ring finger along his scar, his touch appearing to be as gentle as if he were caressing an eggshell. "You don't want to go to County, holmes," he said. "I got this in County."

His tone wasn't menacing or proud. It was a simple fact. It carried a certain detached bemusement, the way an animal who'd been caught in a trap too many times might communicate to a younger animal that they may want to watch their step.

I got the hell out of that jail and vowed never to go back, for any reason at all.

I never did go to County. The judge gave me summary probation, I was sent to alcohol school, and forced with the sobering prospect of being busted for another DUI, I did the smart thing: I swore off driving for life.

Cellphones are another appliance that many in this world take for granted, and in Los Angeles they're the modern equivalent of pants. Walking down the street in just your underwear will garner the same looks you'll get if you're talking on a payphone, whose ranks are growing alarmingly thinner by the year.

In a town like L.A., where people are often forced to engage in conversation with people they don't particularly like, cellphones can be a Godsend. Example:

Two studio execs are droning through a stilted exchange at some outdoor bistro. Cell phone SHRILLS.

Draw! Both execs reach for their cellphones at once. The triumphant one comes up with theirs, gives a studied frown at the caller ID. Then clucks: "I told them not to call me… this'll just take a second… hello… oh…" Looks up at Exec #2 and says: "Sorry, I've got to take this."

Exec #2 nods, understanding, then uses the lull to check *their* cellphone. Given enough interruptions and distractions, cellphones make it possible for two people who really don't want to talk to one another to have a lunch meeting while barely saying four direct words to each other.

Also, cellphones provide status. I'm not talking about those ridiculously small cellphones that are all the rage in Japan and London, the type that are so small they look like prizes one might find in a box of breakfast cereal. In L.A., it's all about quantity. I once saw someone pile three cellphones and a Blackberry onto a table when he sat down at a local pub. I felt a curious desire to ask him why he needed all that hardware.

"You must be important," I commented. When dealing with L.A. citizens, always aim for the vanity.

He laughed. A direct hit.

Far from being defensive, this man seemed almost proud as he explained to me that he had one phone for business, one phone for personal, another for his out-of-town girlfriend, and the Blackberry for when the phones didn't have coverage. It was an impressive setup. Standing there, with no cellphone to call my own, I admit I felt a bit inadequate. Then again, being that I didn't have any friends and worked primarily at home, I didn't have the need to be too accessible. My first five years in Los Angeles, the only urgent call I received was from an old high school friend at three in the morning. "I don't know what the fuck I'm doing with my life!" he wailed.

"Who does?" I asked, before placing the phone snugly under one pillow and going back to bed to the sound of his muffled sobs.

The only component of the cellphone era I can really get my head around is the earpiece. I first saw one of these while shopping at my local supermarket. As I coasted into the beverage section I came upon a woman in a sharply tailored suit trying to decide on a bottle of wine. From her appearance and demeanor she appeared to be an upwardly mobile person, with one wonderful exception: she was having an animated conversation with herself about which bottle of wine she should choose.

Relief swam over me. Suddenly I wasn't the only person who strolled down the street and argued out loud with myself about everything from politics to the merits of playing *Halo* for four hours at a stretch. Here was another seemingly normal person indulging in an argument with whoever might be rattling around inside her head. I studied her carefully as she engaged in a heated debate with some unknown entity about whether or not white wine was appropriate for something called a "disengagement party."

"She'll drink more white wine," she maintained to herself. "And she'll forget how stupid she was to ever get engaged in the first place."

This woman was turning into my potential soulmate. I strolled over and coughed. "Pardon me, my dear…" I began. "But I couldn't help but notice you're talking to—"

She turned to face me, and that's when I saw the earpiece and microphone reaching down across her chin. I recoiled. The mechanized appendage gave her the appearance of a Borg[10].

"You're actually talking to another real person?" I asked. From the look she gave me I didn't know who was more alarmed: her or me.

"Hold on, Martha," she said into the earpiece, then tilted it away. "Not that it's any of your business, but yes, I am. Now what is it you want?"

"Nothing, I just… I thought you were talking to yourself. Or someone…" I floundered. "You know, imaginary."

She frowned. "Do I look like a nutcase to you?" she asked.

Well, no. But I'd been hoping she was one. Nutcases can be easy to come by in Los Angeles, but nutcases that are capable of savoring the virtues of a good bottle of

---

10   A cybernetic organism that occupies the *Star Trek* universe and whose goal it is to assimilate all unique species into their "collective," thus erasing all traces of originality. Well known for their motto, "Resistance is futile."

wine can be few and far between. "Sorry," I said, then blundered on: "I just want to say that I think getting engaged is stupid, as well."

She recoiled a bit, then pointedly spoke into the earpiece loudly: "No, Martha. Just some freak who was eavesdropping on me."

That was my introduction to the earpiece connection.

The next day I went out and bought one, and now I can walk around my neighborhood rambling to myself about the latest book I've read or which season the series *Beverly Hills 90210* officially jumped the shark, and when people pass me we'll often exchange a simple smile of acknowledgement. No longer a person with possible bipolar and/or schizophrenic tendencies, I'm now a proud 21st Century inhabitant that's important enough to not even have the time to walk without being on the phone.

Real cellphones do have their disadvantages, in that liberal use of them can get one into trouble. A friend of mine was out at a party and she took a picture of herself on her phone because she'd just gotten it that day and it was new and she wanted to see if the photo feature worked.

The only problem was she took this inaugural photo of herself making out with some random guy. The next day she'd forgotten about the photo and didn't remember until it surfaced months later when her husband borrowed her phone and was flipping through her photo collection in hopes of finding ones she'd snapped of their three year old child's first time on a swing.

They're still together and, like many married couples in L.A., making a marriage counselor rich.

There's a beauty to being carless and cellless in L.A. I've grown to enjoy the looks of astonishment my fellow Angelenos give me when I inform them I have neither of these objects. More often than not they follow up by offering to loan me money.

But when looked at from a certain skewed point of view, cellphones, known as cells, are just that. With their implied accessibility, this means anyone should be able to reach you, anytime. "Where were you? I tried you on your cell but you didn't pick up!" This is an accusation I never want leveled at me. Truthfully, I enjoy my solitude, and if I'm in the midst of a productive period of writing and/or drinking, I prefer to screen my calls and then when I return them make up a pleasantly white lie about being at the gym.

A friend who lives in Manhattan once commented to me, "It's easy to live without a car in Manhattan. In L.A., it must take some doing." Indeed it does, but that's part of the appeal. Unlike Manhattan, where the only challenge to not owning a car is figuring out what to do with the six hundred dollars a month you don't have to spend on a parking space for it, L.A. provides a sprawling landscape not suited to those without wheels. There used to be a fantastic public transportation service back in the fifties, with trolleys and buses branching out everywhere. However, this system proved too successful and was systematically dismantled by oil, tire, and automobile companies with friends in high places.

So while most people in L.A. own cars, I see not driving in this town as a challenge. Riding a bike keeps me in shape. Taking a bus keeps me in touch with our fair city's citizens. It reminds me of the bus rides to and from junior high school; the most action always happens in the rear of the bus. I've met gang members, people who claim to be being tailed by the C.I.A., men dressed in rags who profess to be worth millions of dollars… the characters are endless.

Occasionally I'll do "rideabouts," where I get on a bus, pay my dollar twenty-five, then sip my Vodkarade while listening to music, writing, and watching Los Angeles go by. There's no better way to see the city. Bret Easton Ellis once wrote, "People are afraid to merge in Los Angeles." Maybe so, but bus drivers certainly aren't. From the Valley to Chinatown to Beverly Hills, I can cruise in the back of a fifteen ton limousine without worry of a DUI, a sudden rear end collision, or an "urgent" phone call from a girlfriend or my crazy Aunt Muriel. Meanwhile, below me, cars are filled with people yammering into cellphones about how horrible traffic is.

I drift above, untraceable, content, a drink in one hand and a pen in the other.

This is freedom in Los Angeles.

THE ARMIES OF THE DAWN
Debauchery as an Essayed Poem
The Essayed Poem as Debauchery

It started, as most misadventures do, with a phone in one hand and a cocktail in the other.

The date was December 11th, 2008. America had just elected a new President, and the times were, in Bob Dylan's words, "a-changin'." Hopefully, anyway, with the economy in tatters, a recession blossoming and a depression knocking.

I awoke at 7:20 in the morning and opened the blinds of my apartment. There was evidence outside of the morning sun slowly climbing, but I needed to confirm that the world was still turning, so I logged onto the Internet. Reassured at the sight of my home page, I poured myself a hair of the mastiff that had bit me last night, then settled down to think up a good idea for a novel that would sell millions of copies worldwide, become a movie, and help teenage outcasts feel better about themselves.

After twenty fruitless minutes, I gave up and settled on writing an immortal poem about revolution on my Facebook page.

An hour and two cocktails later, I'd gotten two words down: "Good revolutionists…"

But what defined a good revolutionist was as elusive to me as what termed luck positive. There's a well told tale about how seemingly good luck and seemingly bad luck may travel through one's life, breaking a young man's leg while at the same time sparing him from having to go to war. Good, bad… with enough life lived they become mere words… important words, yes, but words open to interpretation.

Good revolutionists…

The phone rang.

Norman Mailer once referred to answering his own telephone as sharpening his instinct as a gambler, and I'd always considered myself a gambler.

"Hell-*o*," I answered.

It was a telemarketer by the name of Stephanie, and she was interested in telling me all about how the miserable economy could actually allow me to refinance and therefore save me a ton of money on my mortgage.

I explained that I lived in an apartment. A room, actually. "Where on earth did you get the idea that I owned a house?" I asked, fearing identity theft.

"Oh, they just have these random lists of numbers for us to call," she said. "I'm sorry to have bothered you."

No problem, I assured her while sipping my drink. I added that she sounded like a beautiful young woman and inquired as to exactly where she was calling from.

To my surprise she actually answered me. Phoenix, Arizona, it turned out. I mentioned to her that I was a writer, having written a novel and poetry, and from there things fell forebodingly into place.

We exchanged Facebook links, and when I found her profile I saw she was cute, twenty-three, and a self-described "revolutionist who was ready to march into Washington and show Junior who was really in charge."

I asked her if "Junior" was a reference to our then current President with an approval rating of around 22%. She confirmed that it was.

"We're gonna have a march on the Pentagon in three days," she said. "It'd be cool if you showed up. We could use you as a speaker. You said you were a poet, right?"

Absolutely, I assured her. I mentioned my lack of fear regarding speaking in front of people and titillated Stephanie with tales of my latest poetry reading, telling her there had been 1,014 attendees, thus exaggerating the number of attendees by around a thousand or so.

Stephanie told me she could meet me in Phoenix, if I could get a connecting flight, and then we would fly out to D.C. together. I had plenty of frequent flyer miles and two free weeks ahead of me. I clicked on my airline's website and found a ticket to D.C. with a ninety minute layover in Phoenix. I got the same flight as her to D.C., all the while thinking that the Internet sure made revolution easy these days.

But revolution, as I was to learn, could always retain a sense of complexity. Just like a poem. Still, I was hooked. The only thing, I knew, was to follow the tail of this poem's comet through to the end.

After I hung up the phone, it occurred to me I'd forgotten to ask Stephanie exactly what it was we'd be marching for or against. I assumed it was an anti-war demonstration of some kind, and I was fine with that. I always have and always will be in support of the men and women who serve America, but I did question Junior's decision to send them to a hellhole like Iraq, ostensibly to find "weapons of mass destruction." Though not a single of these supposed WMDs had yet been found, Junior had managed to finish what his father started and knock Saddam Hussein out of the picture, pump billions of dollars into his vice-president's "former" company, while costing thousands of American and Iraqi lives in the process.

I sat up straight in my chair. Five minutes after making a decision to march and I was already fortifying my position. I took a slight sip of my drink and found that first stanza I'd been searching for.

Good revolutionists fight to the bone
Bad   revolutionists   just   answer   the phone

There was a time when you could carry full bottles of vodka in your luggage on planes, but due to morons who slaughter people in the name of fanaticism masquerading as religion, these days are no more. Instead of paying six dollars per drink in the air, the frugal minded traveler buys their cocktails at a liquor store for a dollar per miniature bottle. Since L.A. to D.C. is a nearly four hour flight, I had two dozen "airline sized" bottles of vodka stuffed in my carry on luggage.

Adaptation. It's what's helped make America great.

I was a bit anxious on .the flight to Phoenix. Here I'd met this woman over the phone and was now flying across the country with her to engage in some sort of protest. But what woman in their right mind would pick up a total stranger over the phone? At least, being a guy, I had a decent excuse for allowing myself to be seduced by a total stranger over the phone.

As far as her attractive Facebook photo went, it was possible she'd posted a picture of her hot friend or even some random pic she'd cut and pasted from another website. I drowned out these possibilities with four miniature bottles of vodka on the plane. We landed, deplaned, and I looked about the gate area for Steph.

"Mister Michals!"

I turned and was relieved to see that Stephanie was, amazingly, very similar to her Facebook photos. Dimples. Long flowing red hair. Eyes that sparked with the promise of all kinds of revolutionary experiences. She seemed almost too beautiful to be a revolutionist, given that she probably could be making thousands a night working as an escort for politicians. What the hell was she doing trying to overthrow a system like that?

When I asked Stephanie this, she just laughed and replied she didn't want to overthrow it, just shake it up a little.

"I think I love you," I told her.

"Partridge Family, nineteen-seventy," she smiled.

I was suitably impressed. "Now I know I love you." I said. "I'm a believer!"

She shrieked excitedly. "The Monkees! They ruled!"

I took her by the hand. "Let's get our first kiss over with, shall we?"

Stephanie was agreeable enough, and we went into a clinch. Two revolutionists with a thing for cheesy T.V. bands making out in Terminal B of the Phoenix airport. Our fellow travelers passed us without batting an eye.

That done, we hurried to our gate to fly into history.

There was a problem, though, when the gate attendants performed a spot check on my bag and found my vodka bottles. "I'm sorry, sir," one of them said. "We can't let you through with all these."

"But I just flew from L.A. with all of them." I protested.

The guy was tall, with a mole on the left side of his lip. He looked like a reasonable enough person, and there was regret in his voice as he said, "I'm sorry, sir. But there's just too many of them."

He seemed to be trying to hold back a chuckle.

"But it's a long flight," I pointed out. "My fiancé and I are going to Washington D.C. to change history."

I put my arm around my newly christened fiancée, and she kissed my cheek.

"We can let you take ten of them," he said. "But we've got to keep the other ten."

"Fair enough," I allowed. "Have yourselves a party."

"Oh no, sir," he said. "We're going to destroy them, not drink them."

I was aghast. "You don't mean you're going to let perfectly good vodka go to waste?"

"I'm afraid we have to."

"Damn, man!" I exhaled. "That's a sin. You don't mind if my fiancé and I have a few before we get on, do you?"

He looked around. The only people for him to look to were two other attendants, both older and both now openly laughing.

"Go ahead, I suppose," he said, pausing before every word, nervous as a government official denying something.

I immediately uncapped one of the airline bottles and drained it. When I was done, I was pleased to see that Stephanie had managed to down another of the bottles just as quickly.

"Wow," I said, "You may be my dream girl."

"The liver is a very sensitive organ in our chakra," Stephanie told me. "We need to prepare ours for anything."

Though it sounded like nothing more than an excuse to uncap another bottle, I managed to nod seriously enough before doing so. By this time the gate attendants were in hysterics.

"Gosh dang!" one of them howled. "You can't get on a plane like that!"

But we did. And if any terrorists were watching, no doubt the sight of two people chugging vodka at the gate was enough to convince them that this was a flight that was perhaps worth skipping. When drunk, people tend to take life either way more or way less seriously. Certainly a person who has a few under their belt is more likely to launch themselves at a terrorist, results be damned. Not out of any patriotic duty or even a sense of humanity; it's just that, as has been so eloquently stated, drunkards are "citizens of the world." And the world, especially when seen through a few stiff martinis, is worth fighting for.

Good revolutionists try to locate the chakra
Bad revolutionists try to locate the vodka

We located the vodka, all right, we located it all throughout the flight. We also managed to locate each other's tongues and crotches. I'm sure we thought we were doing so discreetly, but our moans might've given us away. I certainly did feel for the poor guy who was sitting in the window seat beside us, but I explained at selected intervals during the flight that we were newlyweds, and he seemed accepting of this. The flight attendants cast a few curious glances at us, which made me feel an unreasonable guilt. Surely a display of affection on a plane shouldn't be a crime.

Good revolutionists invoke social change
Bad revolutionists make out on the plane

Overall the flight was certainly pleasant. Eight airline-sized bottles of vodka perished at its hands. As Stephanie and I were disembarking a flight attendant approached us.

"You two are really something," she clucked.

Stephanie looked a bit panicked, so I took the lead. ""We broke no laws," I stated. "And we're in love."

The flight attendant laughed. "I just wanted to give you this," she said, holding out a bottle of champagne. "And say congratulations."

"On what?" I asked, confused.

"Your engagement," she said. "You were announcing it to the whole plane."

I had no memory of this. This was unnerving, but the flight attendant holding out the bottle of champagne was reassuring. I took it and thanked her.

As we walked out of the terminal we were greeted by a tall thin man with a five o'clock shadow and a Che Guevara t-shirt.

"Hey, sis!" he hooted, grabbing Stephanie into a hug.

Introductions were made. His name was Carl, and he was Stephanie's brother, older by four years. "So you're the poet," he greeted me.

"When I get drunk enough," I assured him. "I'm the greatest poet alive."

"Terrific!" he clapped. "You'll be the Master of Ceremonies at the pre-march rally tonight."

Master of Ceremonies. This sounded like a position that required way more responsibility than someone like me could exhibit. Not to mention decorum, class, etc. But with the way Stephanie was looking at me, my ego felt like the Grinch's heart on Christmas morning when he heard the Whos singing down in Whoville. And to anyone who knows me and is therefore aware that my ego is already freakishly huge, the idea of it growing several sizes is an alarming concept.

"It would be an honor and a privilege," I bowed to Carl.

Ten minutes later we were coasting out of the short-term parking area. "Here," Carl said, fishing out a flask. "Grey Goose vodka in there with a splash of Clamato Juice, Tabasco, Worchester, and a bit of dill sprinkled in."

"Never had a Caesar from a flask before,"
I said, taking the flask.

"We gays know how to mix a drink,
honey," he answered.

From the backseat Stephanie flashed me
a smile. Well, her brother was gay. That
was all right. I took a swig and passed
the flask back to him. "So just where are
these ceremonies I'm supposed to be the
master of tonight?" I asked.

"A bar," he nodded, swerving around a
construction worker waving a sign marked
SLOW. "It's called the Oral Orifice."

I choked a bit, the Tabasco in my throat
abruptly making its presence known. "That
sounds… like a gay bar or something," I
said.

"It is." Carl said. "What do you think
this protest march is about?"

"I thought… you know, ending the Iraqi
war."

Stephanie and Carl both howled in
laughter. "Hell no," Carl's pronuncia-
tion of "hell" managed to make it sound
as if the word had at four separate syl-
lables. "It's about our right to *serve* in
the war. As a Republican, I feel that if
my country's at war, I should be allowed
to serve, regardless of my sexuality."

Ye Gods. I'd never met a Gay Republican. To me they'd always seemed a completely self-contradictory species. Kind
of like a duck who believed in hunting.

"I'm bisexual," Stephanie piped up from the backseat. "And I want to serve, too."

"But don't Republicans think gay people are, like, evil?" I asked.

"Two hundred years ago, didn't Americans think African Americans were, like, slaves?" Carl asked. His tone was pointed with a thin icing of mockery. "And we're going to be inaugurating our first African-American president in two weeks."

I had to admit he had a point. A good point.

We celebrated Carl's good point with another round of sips from the flask. On the drive in Carl talked a bit about his past. He'd been a bounty hunter, a stuntman, and had literally broken a ball as a child when he'd leapt on the railing of a fence from a roof during a game of tag.

"They had to remove it," Carl said. "But the good news is my other testicle's actually grown bigger. Compensation, the doctors say."

"Hmm..." I said, finishing off the flask. "Wish I had two livers."

"Wish I had four tits," Stephanie laughed.

"So do I!" Carl hooted.

I almost asked if he was wishing for tits for him or for his sister. But I didn't dare delve into these specifics and instead just laughed along with him and his sister. My new comrades.

Good revolutionists seek traditions to shatter
Bad revolutionists wish for more body matter

Carl and Stephanie had managed to secure an apartment in a building located in a fairly posh section of D.C. Trees lined the streets and the air itself smelled of a lushness born from tradition. If a mugger were to confront you on these streets, it felt as if a simple "Don't you know where you *are,* my good man?" could send them slinking away into the night, ashamed at their presumptuousness.

All around us people were strolling about, dining on restaurant patios and appearing as though they didn't have a care in the world. I don't know what I'd expected. Maybe more concerned looks, maybe characters walking along with purpose as though they'd just wandered in from an episode of *The West Wing,* which I'd always thought was both inspiring and pathetic in that the show demonstrated how far Hollywood could raise the bar for reality.

It occurred to me that Washington D.C. could almost be the East Coast's answer to Los Angeles. They shared a common insular quality. The outside world may be suffering, but when one arrived at a film premiere or a dinner to honor some ambassador, one would never know it. Both towns seem run by power, money, sex, and above all, illusion. In twenty-first century America movie stars and politicians have undergone a blending, adopting interchangeable limits that they are measured by. Both roles now involve sitting down at a table that serves all the sexual scandals, public performances and chances for one's star to rise meteorically and crash spectacularly. After 9/11, Junior had an unprecedented approval rating. Now, seven years later, he'd made disastrous choices and his ratings were in the toilet. He'd obviously chosen the wrong roles to play, that of a cowboy who wanted to "chase them out of the foxholes," without knowing who "they" were or where the "foxholes" were. He'd chosen to play a war hero who pronounced "mission accomplished" when not only had very little been accomplished but the mission *itself* had been unclear at best.

Back when Hollywood was rising, a screenwriter named Herman Mankiewicz had sent his friend and fellow writer Ben Hecht a telegram saying, "Millions are to be grabbed out here and your only competition is idiots." With the kind of money flow in D.C., what with all the cash pouring in from taxes and lobbyists and campaign contributions to all the pork and earmarks that sharp ~~hustlers~~ Congressmen can steer their way, couldn't Hecht have also been describing our nation's capital?

I put this theory to Stephanie and Carl as we arrived at our destination and headed through the lobby, our footsteps echoing against the marble walls, making our entry sound as important as a judge's gavel.

"You're a deep thinker," Stephanie said, in that overly flattering tone someone uses when they really want you to shut up.

"I'm a better drinker," I assured her.

Good revolutionists believe in the right to think

Bad revolutionists believe in having another drink

The apartment was hardwood, with porcelain chandeliers. A musty odor permeated the living room, which had two couches and a weathered American flag above the fireplace. Black and white pictures in elaborate frames lined shelves on either side of the flag. They appeared to be arranged in a timeline of sorts, showing a man grown progressively chunkier over the years shaking hands with every U.S. President since Richard Nixon. "Who's this joker?" I asked.

"A Congressman. This is one of the apartments he uses for his, ahem, indiscretions."

"Does he know we're here?" I asked, not so buzzed that I couldn't envision a group of dark-suited men crashing through the door and taking us into custody.

"Honey, you need to relax," Stephanie said, sidling up to me. "You've got to be *on* for that big speech tonight, remember?"

"Right," I nodded. "This being a love nest, I suppose there's something to drink around here, right?"

"Remember this?" Stephanie flashed the bottle of champagne at me, the one the flight attendant had given us to celebrate our engagement I'd fabricated.

"Beautiful," I said.

Stephanie popped it open and licked the bubbly as it foamed over the top. I joined her. Then she took me by the hand and led me into the bedroom.

"That's not the only thing that's gonna explode around here, baby," Stephanie whispered.

Good revolutionists say all you need is love
Bad revolutionists know all you need's a glove

A couple hours later I was drained, rested, showered, and sipping a cocktail on our way to the venue for the night's ceremonies.

"That apartment we're staying in is totally safe," Carl was saying. "The Congressman's been married for twenty-four years. He and his wife have a, shall we say, understanding."

"He gets to have sex with prostitutes," I suggested.

"That and she gets to have her pick of his young interns. As they say in Washington, all in the family."

"How do you know so much about this?"

"Hell, I was one of the interns."

"You had sex with the Congressman's wife?" I asked.

Carl nodded. Stephanie was smoking pot in the backseat, humming along to Bob Dylan's "Rainy Day Women" that was crooning from the Make a Difference channel on Satellite Radio.

"But you're… gay." I said to Carl. "Right?"

"Honey," he sighed. "At the time, *I* wanted to be a Congressman. I would've screwed Swiss cheese if it had got me there."

Stephanie's hum was cut off by her laughter. She passed the pipe up to Carl, who took a hit and held it out to me.

"No thanks," I said, holding up my drink. "I'm an old fashioned kind of guy."

"Come on, do a narc hit."

"Narc hit?"

"Yeah," Stephanie chirped from the back. "So we know you're not a narc."

How these people thought I'd take a random flight from L.A. just to bust them smoking a bowl of pot made no sense to me, but I chalked it up to stoner's paranoia on their part and took a hit.

I inhaled the sweet smoke and exhaled smoothly.

"So you used to want to be a Congressman," I said to Carl. "What do you want to be now?"

He paused, passing streetlights speckling his face. "Honest," he said.

Good revolutionists try to save the whale
Bad revolutionists make sure to inhale

The Oval Orifice was packed. Strangely, for the most part it looked like a bar one would find in the Midwest. Farm tools were displayed on the walls. In the middle of the dance floor was a rusted tractor. Pictures of sports teams lined the walls alongside neon beer signs. The dress was mostly blue jeans and cowboy boots. The jukebox had Toby Keith singing about Stars and Stripes and where eagles flew.

The only glaring variable that separated this bar from its Middle American counterparts were the strips of rainbow colored paper spelled out "FREEDOM" on the ceiling.

No sooner had I downed my first drink and gotten over my Urban Cowboy flashback when I found myself being pushed up on stage with an introduction by Carl that sounded something like… "the sexiest writer since John Rechy and the drunkest writer since Charles Bukowski…"

I grabbed the microphone before I could be vaulted up to any more standards. A thought came to me, not the first time it would come that weekend, that to be the President of the United States must in so many ways be a terrible burden. After all, here I was, a writer who had just had only one book published, and still I was feeling pressure in this town to fill shoes of all those who had come before me.

Writers, as important as we may be in that books are capable of bringing change, are no match for presidents.

Applause bubbled up, and I realized I'd actually spoken that line. I also realized I was fairly stoned. Though I can consume vodka basically from the time I get up to the time I pass out and still function at least halfway normally, one hit of marijuana and I usually spend it huddled in a corner of my apartment, headphones on while making short work of a large pizza from Papa John's.

But here I was, no apartment, no head-phones, no large pizza. Just a sea of people awaiting my next words. There was nothing for it but to venture on. But being that I suddenly had a suspicion that the place might be bugged, I had to be careful not to say anything too incen-diary or incriminating.

"In just a few weeks we will see the first African-American president of this country," I said. More applause. "And I think the world needs this. The world needs change. And this country, more than most, seems ready to embrace change."

A few boos broke out. "Ask California!" "Prop Eight!" "Where are our rights?"

"Your rights are here!" I shouted, accepting a glass of something from Stephanie. "You didn't ask to be gay, did you?"

A silence accentuated only by the flick-ing of lighters to light cigarettes, in blatant disregard of the no-smoking ordi-nance that seems to be in effect every-where.

"Did you ask to be gay?" I shouted, then took a big swallow from the glass Stephanie had handed me. I spit it out. Water.

"No!" a few shouts came from the crowd.

"Of course not," I said. "Who would want to be made fun of, spat upon, ostra-cized, and basically told you're walking proof of natural selection, given that you'll never have kids."

"Right!" "Say it!" "Preach!"

"I know what you're going through," I went on. "I know because I'm one of you."

Whoops from the crowd.

"I'm a writer," I went on, the drink and marijuana swirling around within me, creating a hurricane. I looked over to Stephanie and she blew me a kiss. My ego blossomed another five sizes. "Not just any writer," I babbled on. "But the proud holder of the belt that Mister Hemingway and Mister Fitzgerald once held. I pinned Mister Hemingway with my first unpublished novel. Then I went on to beat Mister Fitzgerald by disqualification with my second novel, published, by the way." Here I gave the title and a quick synopsis, my paranoia retreating in direct relation to my blatant self-promotion.

"Are you a homo?" someone from the crowd shouted.

"I am who I am!" I shot back. "I didn't choose to be a writer. You didn't choose to be homosexuals! It's *who we are!"*

I looked to the side of the stage where Carl and Stephanie were standing. Their faces shone with pleasant bewilderment. I'd been seeking firmer expressions, ones of either rabid approval or distaste. However, given that they'd smoked a hell of a lot more pot than I had, their con-fused looks were explainable.

I looked back to the crowd, which seemed to be growing restless. "Do you suck dick?" someone shouted.

I was losing my audience. But then in a flash of drunken semi-stoned brilliance an idea came to me. Name recognition. The twenty-first century was already filled with politicians and celebrities whose sole qualification for being in their appointed posts seemed to be their last names and the public's ability to infuse those names with meaning.

I shouted out my last name. It was a last name that I'd considered a pseudonym ever since I'd been disowned by the abu-sive man who had thankfully taken himself out of the running as my real dad. Still, I'd kept the name because I'd always thought it would make a nice chant say, on *The Tonight Show* or at a Superbowl halftime concert. Why not try it out in a gay bar in our nation's capital?

But as I chanted my last name repeat-edly, people in this very real audience only exchanged uncomfortable looks with each other.

"Eat my ass, honey!" a drag queen down front shouted.

"You come up here, sweetie," I responded. "I'll *marry* you!"

This unleashed a wave of cheers. Within seconds I was face to face with a pink haired being who looked strikingly like a woman in her faded blue jeans, boots, tube-top, and Stetson. The only flaws in the slaw were the patch of fuzz underneath her bottom lip and the undeniable fact that she was chewing tobacco.

Just a month ago I'd been having a debate with the husband of one of my cousins in which he'd termed homosexuals a "scourge on the earth" and wished "every one of them to burn in hell." I'd seized upon the opportunity to announce to him that not only had I had my dick sucked by dozens of guys in my life (a slight exaggeration) but that I was bisexual and planning to get married to a man.

Though I really had no intention of ever getting married to anyone, man, woman, or beast, when presented with the opportunity to both offend an in-law and stand up for the rights of others at the same time, I felt mere circumstance justified a white lie.

Now here was a drag queen bowing down before me, offering me her hand in marriage. As I listened to the crowd before us roar their approval, my buzz gave way to a wave of terror. Did these people actually expect me to grow into something I'd only *spoken* about becoming?

Standing there on that stage I suddenly felt a painful stab of empathy for Junior. Hadn't he been cast into something totally over his head after 9/11? He'd been the leader of a free world in which all the rules had horrifically changed. Junior had simply done what he knew would please his father. Get oil. Get Saddam. And like a fortunate son he'd gone for what he knew.

Now, onstage before a mass of homosexuals who evidently were passionate about having the right to kill in the name of God and Country, staring at this bulky drag queen kneeling before me demanding marriage, I found myself going with what *I* knew.

"Drinks all around!" I shouted.

There were cries of joy from those assembled, and I immediately dove into the audience and made my way to the bar, not quite knowing what I was doing, but feeling that, well whatever the hell it was, it was *right. Staying the course,* as Junior would say.

Soon I was doing shooters with Stephanie and my supposed bride-to-be, whose name was a nicely ambiguous Ronni (*with an I,* she winked at me), and was being taught the Achy-Breaky dance. At one point I recall being led to a back room where the walls were coated with red velvet.

Then I blacked out.

Good revolutionists preach against the world's doom
Bad revolutionists black out in the red room

I awoke with my arm around someone. I opened my eyes and closed them quickly.

Either I was still seeing double, or my first glimpse of the day had revealed there were in fact two people in bed with me.

My eyes peeked open again. There was Stephanie, naked. She looked beautiful and seemed to have a satisfied smile on her face. The third person also had a satisfied smile, but this was more disconcerting because it was Ronni with an I, my pink haired "bride" from last night.

I didn't have a ring on my finger, which I took as a good sign. I wasn't sore anywhere, another good sign.

I crept out of bed and after dressing hastily made my way out to the living room. Carl was at his computer, tapping keys and laughing away. "You're a hit, baby!" he called out.

"Cool," I nodded. I had no idea what he was talking about nor did I care. At that moment, all I wanted was to get an eye opener into me as quickly as possible.

I found an almost full bottle of Stoli in the freezer and felt considerably calmer.

A minute later, tumbler in hand, I joined Carl at the computer. He was watching YouTube, laughing like hell. To my surprise there I was onscreen, ranting, declaring myself Heavyweight Champion of the literary world, proposing marriage, and generally making a fool of myself.

"Gahhh…" I sputtered. "Who the hell taped this craziness?"

Carl gave me an amused shrug. "Who the hell *didn't?*" he declared. "There were a ton of people with their cellphones and HD cameras there. Think about it. In the olden days, it would've taken days to get this footage out to the public. But in this present… upload and boom! You're in front of the world. Isn't it grand?"

Grand wasn't exactly the word I felt on the tip of my tongue. *Frightening, horrific, invasive…* any of those would've done nicely in describing the realization that, in this brave new world of imaging cellphones and the Internet, whenever you get a bit out of control in public it's only a matter of a quick upload and then download before millions can witness your antics. In the old days my performance from last night would've been lucky to make it into the free weekly paper. But here I was on YouTube, onstage, raving for all to see. My heart went out, again, to the politicians of modern times. Back in the day, Franklin Delano Roosevelt had

had the respect of media and the limited
technology of the time had made it possible for him to disguise the fact that
he led the U.S. out of the Great Depression from a wheelchair. In this era, that
would never be possible. Mispronounce the
name of a country, stumble over repeated
sentences, choke on a pretzel… it's all
going to be right there for people to
see.

Poor Junior, I thought. He'd come of
age as a President during the stretch
from years 2000 to 2008. The Internet had
been growing exponentially during that
time, and he'd clearly been a babe in
the woods. How was he to know that when
he spoke about "the Internets," seeing
tides actually turn, and a seemingly endless amount of other times he'd appeared
to be an idiot while on camera, people
would actually be able to view this uned-
ited footage with a few taps of a computer key?

"So… what do you think?" Carl asked
me, replaying my drunken speech from the
night before.

I thought I was happy most of my relatives didn't have a computer and I
thanked God I wasn't President of the
United States.

"'Morning all!" Ronni announced, emerging from the bedroom. She was back in her
outfit from the night before. "Oh honey,

you and Stephanie were just del-licious last night."

"Um... Ronni..." I said. "Hold on,"

I slammed the rest of the tumbler. There had to be around a half-pint of vodka in there, and I needed it to brace myself for the possible answer to my next question.

"We aren't married... are we?"

Ronni sighed and tweaked my cheek. "Darlin', let me just say this. If we'd gotten married last night, I would've consummated with you. And let me assure *you,* that if that had happened, you'd feel it."

With the flourish of a prosecuting attor-ney whipping out a key piece of evidence, Ronni revealed her genitalia. I was suit-ably impressed and a bit horrified at how close I'd conceivably gotten to becoming intimate with that thing. "Wow," I said. In the words of Richard Price, one of the authors I hadn't last night boasted about beating in my inexorable climb to the top of the writing world, Ronni's member "wasn't only big, it was as thick as a woman's wrist."

Carl whistled. "You could put an eye out with that thing!"

Ronni holstered her weapon and blew us both a kiss. "I'll see you cuties at the march. And I swear, if I don't get the right to join the army and kill me some enemies of the state, I'll just…" Ronni sighed and straightened herself in a dignified fashion. "I don't know what I'll do."

No sooner had Ronni strolled confidently out of the apartment, whistling a vaguely patriotic melody, when Stephanie swept in from the bedroom.

"Hey, big bro." she said to Carl, then sidled up to me. "Well, hi there, husband of mine."

I spit out the mouthful of vodka I was swallowing. "Husband?"

"Yes, silly," Stephanie chuckled. "We got married last night. Now don't tell me you don't remember."

"I remember being at the bar…" I said.

"You don't remember charging up onto the stage. I was in the middle of reciting my poem about why I hate straight men. You got on your knees and offered apologies on behalf of the whole heterosexual male species. And then you proposed to me. You gave me this," she flashed a plastic ring that had a big lollipop in the place of a jewel. All the while I was going through vague recollections of the night before and thinking to myself, *Yes, yes that is something a drunken me would do.*

Stephanie was going on. "One of the guys there was an ordained minister," she said. "He married us. We had some pretty unique vows, but it's official. We're hitched."

"Mom and Dad'll be thrilled. They were afraid she'd turn into an old maid." Carl cackled, and Stephanie gave him a playful slap on the left temple.

Marriage. Foreign territory, with absolutely no idea how to proceed.

The only way to proceed, I reasoned as I finished my drink, was to do just that. Keep going forward with this craziness. Stay the fucking course. "Baby," I grabbed Stephanie. "I love you."

We kissed for a second, then she pulled away. "My God, you taste like vodka!" she exclaimed.

"Yes," I replied, making my way back to the kitchen. "And in a few minutes, I'm going to taste like it a lot more."

Good revolutionists protest the world's troubles
Bad revolutionists just pour themselves doubles

We got to the area of the march at about eleven in the morning. I had my trusty Diet Mountain Dew bottle, half-filled with vodka, and was swigging liberally. I'd forgone my regular Vodkarade because I figured it was going to be a long day and I'd need the caffeine content from the Dew. About twenty yards away were a row of barriers. Beyond them were Federal Marshals. Most of them seemed to be wearing expressions of amazement, if not downright amusement and good cheer.

Outside the barriers, bikers in leather vests and chaps mingled with guys who looked like they'd stepped out of a copy of *GQ* and women who could've been on the cover of an issue of *Good Housekeeping.* Drag queens kibitzed with portly men in three piece suits.

"Do you think all these people are gay?" I asked Stephanie.

"Probably not all," she said. "Some are parents, others are just people like you." She gave me a wink. "You are straight… or aren't you?"

The last time I'd been seriously questioned about my sexuality was when I'd visited the Los Angeles Gay and Lesbian Center Medical Clinic. It had been about a couple years after I'd arrived in Los Angeles, and one of the women I'd picked up in an Internet chatroom had left me with a case of genital warts. A friend had told me that the L.A. Gay and Lesbian Center would treat them for a donation of "as much as I could afford," as opposed to the eight hundred dollars a hospital would charge. Being that I was temping and had no health insurance, I took a bus to the center and filled out a bunch of forms. One of the questions on the forms was related to my sexuality and had different boxes labeled *Gay, Straight, Bisexual, Transgender,* or *Undecided.* The instructions indicated I was to check one. I had the paranoid delusion that marking the *Straight* box would make them delay my treatment, so I chose *Undecided.* It was an ignorant assumption on my part, and I later learned when speaking to the doctor that they treated everyone regardless of their sexuality. I felt stupid for jumping to conclusions, and wound up donating for their treatment my entire food budget for the week, which was around forty dollars.

That week, living on vodka, cigarettes, and whatever food I could steal from the salad bar at the Carl's Jr. down the block from my apartment, I pondered that *Undecided* box I'd checked. I considered myself to be semi-erudite and could pop off a bon mot with the best of them. Leather pants always appealed to me over blue jeans. I loved ABBA, and had once done a striptease to "Dancing Queen" at a bar in Santa Monica. During my years in L.A., more than a couple of my girlfriends had proposed that my considerable intake of alcohol served to cover up latent homosexual desires.

Of course, one look at the squalid mess that was my apartment squashed most people's suggestions that I was homosexual in any way. "Homosexual men wouldn't last a minute in here," one of my girlfriends had said, her tone hovering between confusion and relief.

Yet here I was now, outside a government building, standing side by side among homosexuals demanding to be allowed to serve in a war I didn't even agree with. I suppose I was as undecided as ever.

In spite of the helicopters in the sky, policemen on horseback, and the MPs wearing gas masks and visors, the atmosphere retained a festive air. Our numbers weren't big, maybe three thousand at the most, a pittance as far as marches go. This gathering seemed almost more like a really large party than a protest.

As the clock approached noon, the event seemed in danger of flattening out. Like the lulls that come at parties, where people are over the initial excitement of arrival and ready to shift into another gear but not knowing how. The truth about parties is that they are always at risk of becoming tired dull affairs, too many people agreeing on too much, retelling stories that have already been told. One of my day jobs back when I'd first moved to L.A. had been as a "professional ice-breaker." I'd been paid twenty dollars an hour to be in attendance at corporate parties and circulate, breaking the ice between those from Finance and those from Personnel. Since most of these various camps often disliked one another, this was no simple task. But still, as long as there was an open bar, it was easy enough to get a little whacky and thus they bonded in their mutual horror at some of my antics like heckling the boss when he made a speech during the party. Or if there was a hypnotist I'd be the one to volunteer to get hypnotized, then proceed to make a willing fool of myself by barking like a dog under his "command," etc. Hell, somebody had to play the clown, and I was damn good at it.

Today would prove to be no exception, I determined, as I had another swallow of my vodkaed-down Diet Mountain Dew and began to saunter toward the barricade. I'd come on this adventure for experience, after all.

"Where are you going, honey?" Stephanie called to me, running up to my side.

"I'm going to get arrested." I said, and was happy to find that this declaration revealed an honest desire. Last night, hadn't I taken the bold and drunken step of declaring myself the Literary Champion of the World? It seemed I at least owed the world an experience worth writing about.

Stephanie wrapped her arms around me and gave me a long kiss. "Christ be with you," she whispered in my ear.

Christ was indeed with me. Or at least His blood was. I took another swig and approached the barricades. One of the MPs saw me coming and straightened up.

I stood on one side of the barricade. He was on the other. "Sir, you're not allowed past here," he said.

Behind me I could hear Stephanie beginning a chant that was quickly gaining steam. The sound of my last name filled the air. I was certainly breaking *this* party open. I hadn't had a reaction like this at a party since the time at a studio exec's place when I'd grabbed a popular television actress and simulated giving her oral sex on the dance floor while she looked down at me in horror. The partygoers had loved it, but her bodyguards hadn't. I'd been ejected from the party.

Now, I felt a similar feeling of exhilaration, though the stakes were considerably higher. I was about to commit a federal crime. I wish I could say I had a profound thought or two about how the United States hadn't allowed blacks or women into the military, but had gradually adapted to the fact that people were all different and it was not necessary nor practical to define them by race or sexuality. I wish I could testify that I believed that my actions were in service to my country, that they would break open a time when gay soldiers would save the lives of their fellow soldiers as easily as heterosexual ones could. Or perhaps a gay translator would intercept a message from one terrorist to another and save thousands of lives. I wanted desperately to be entertaining the idea of how amazing America was, that a man who just a hundred and fifty years ago would've been considered a slave would in just two months be our country's President.

However, in truth, all I could focus on was that for the first time in my life people were chanting my name and calling me to action. Even though I considered my last name an alias of sorts, I've always been a sucker for action.

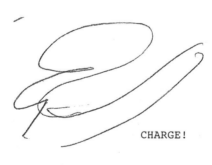

CHARGE!

So as my fictional name rang out behind me from hundreds of throats, I hopped over the barricade and stared at the MP before me. He was probably about my age, maybe a year or two younger. He seemed startled, but his face hadn't lost his trace of amusement. Did he think this was a prank of some kind?

"You don't want to do this," he warned.

His smile irked me; it was the smile of one who doubts another's sincerity.

I made a grab for his crotch in order to distract him, and to my amazement it worked. As he recoiled from my reach, I was able to dodge around him and sprint into no man's land.

"Toodles!" I hooted, shifting my sprint into a skip, thinking that my blatant show of homosexuality might somehow render me immune from further attempted apprehension.

It wasn't somehow so. Within seconds there were hands all over me and forcing me to the ground. "I was just kidding!" I shouted. "I'm not gay! I swear!"

"Sir, we're not arresting you because you're gay—"

"I'm not—"

"You're *trespassing* on Federal grounds, dipshit. Not to mention that you smell as intoxicated as hell."

Oh yeah. Intoxicated as hell dipshit. Now that shoe definitely fit.

Two Marshals straightened me up and led me across the street. To my disappointment they didn't even put me in handcuffs. But at least I was being firmly gripped on each arm by men wearing uniforms and carrying guns. "The revolution has begun!" I shouted. Already more people were starting to climb over the barricades.

"Jesus," one of the Marshals escorting me muttered, and gave my arm a squeeze. "Would you please shut up?"

"Just trying to enliven things," I said. I was tempted to begin shouting *Attica,* but figured that would be ridiculous. Instead I began to shout, "Stonehenge! Stone henge!"

The Marshal to my left looked at me in utter confusion. "What the hell does Stonehenge have to do with this?"

Such ignorance. Well it figured, his being a Federal Marshal. What, I figured drunkenly, would he know about the history of gay rights? I decided to help him out. "That was in New York," I explained. "When gays in America first rebelled against police—"

"That was Stone*wall*," the Marshal replied. He was thin, with a precise moustache. He smelled like aftershave.

"Oh," I replied. "Sorry."

"Are you even gay, for chrissakes?" he asked, sounding strangely offended.

"I'm undecided." I protested.

The two of them led me to a paddy wagon that looked like a black ambulance. I was put inside and told to wait. Given all the action that was starting to take place at the barricades, they didn't have time to frisk me. So I still had my Diet

Mountain Dew bottle, which I sipped from cautiously while able to watch the mounting chaos outside.

There was a lot of motion, bodies darting about, accompanied by a cacophony of chanting and shouts. It looked like a pro wrestling battle royal in which none of the participants knew what the finish was going to be, or even in which order they were supposed to be thrown out of the ring.

After a while, the wagon began to fill up. One of my fellow revolutionaries, a drag queen clad in a sweeping red skirt and hair wrapped in a bun, gave a little shriek when she saw me. "You're that boy!" she said. "From last night at the Oval Orifice."

"Guilty," I said.

"You were a *scream,*" she gushed.

Another revolutionist, this one a husky goateed man with a biker's helmet on, was glaring at me.

"What's up?" I asked him, a bit nervously.

"What the hell are you doing here?" he demanded. "All you did last night on stage was talk about your stupid book. And then you got married to that crazy woman! Why didn't you talk about our right as citizens of this country to serve it? You're not even gay, are you?"

"Why does it matter if I'm gay or not?" I asked him. "What does it matter what *anyone* is? That's what this country, this march is all about, isn't it? Getting the right for all people to defend all people?"

"Amen, honey!" the queen shouted, and a few assorted others who'd been placed in the bus hooted in support.

A loud clang rang out from something hitting the truck. "Too much damn noise in there!" a Marshal shouted from outside.

We quieted down. The biker sneered at the queen and said quietly, "You don't belong in here either, Miss Thing."

In a soft purr the queen asked the biker, "How many people have you killed in your life, honey?"

"Huh?"

The queen placed a hand on the biker's thigh. "Back before I became Regina, I was Reggie," she cooed. "I was in Special Forces as a man, and I killed people. Plenty of 'em."

The biker was shifting nervously. Apparently, underneath his exterior of badass leather clad hellion was someone who was capable of being frightened by an elegantly dressed transsexual.

"You go, girl." I said to Regina.

Good revolutionists see a flaming queen
Bad revolutionists see a killing machine

Once the van was full we were driven to a processing center a few miles away. Besides Reggie and the biker, the only other person who stood out to me was a woman with modestly long hair dressed in army fatigues. Written in lipstick on her cheek was a peace symbol with the word "SUCKS" beneath it.

The rest of the men were normal looking guys, dressed in jeans, khaki pants. Some in cowboy boots and others in loafers. They could've been going to a concert instead of a protest.

We got to the processing center and Marshals escorted each of us off the truck. Since I'd been the first one in, I wound up being the last one out. As I stepped off, the same Marshal who'd led me to the truck gripped my shoulder. "Not you," he said. "The Chief wants to meet you."

I nodded, trapped in a vain attempt to appear calmer than I felt. The Chief? Just that title sounded ominous, kind of like Kurtz in Conrad's *Heart of Darkness.*

On the way through the double doors, where we bypassed processing, I asked my escort what kind of cologne he was wearing.

He looked surprised for a second. "Something blue," he said slowly. "I don't know, it was a gift. Why?"

"It just smells good." I said quickly. *Shit, good move, you homo.* "But I'm not hitting on you or anything. I'm not—"

"Yeah, yeah, I know," he sighed. He murmured something under his breath that sounded a bit like *causeit clean.*

To deny being a "closet queen" would no doubt just cause more complications, so for probably the first time since I'd picked up that damn phone and met Stephanie, I did the smart thing and kept my mouth shut.

We stopped at a large oak door that was slightly ajar. The Marshal gave a light knock. "Come on in, Harold," a voice from within boomed.

Harold and I stepped into a small office. Behind a desk cluttered with papers was a large clean-shaven man, wisps of dark infiltrating his mostly grayed hair. He was painting a model airplane.

"I'll take it from here, Harold. Thanks for bringing him here," The Chief's eyes didn't leave the plane in his hands as he spoke.

"Yes, sir." Harold said. "Should I—"

"Close the door behind you."

I didn't particularly like the sound of that. I looked quickly around the room for a sign, any sign, that I might have a common bond with this man. A small bookcase, a wet bar, a Doors poster… any would have provided comfort. But all I saw were wood paneled walls, on which hung important looking papers that looked like accommodations along with pictures of The Chief with various older men who bore that cheesy smile politicians seem to be able to pull off so well.

I settled on the model airplane he was painting so meticulously. Well, my friends and I had assembled some back when we'd been kids. So that was some sort of bond, right? Then again after we'd hurriedly assembled them we'd stuck firecrackers inside them and launched them off the roofs of our houses so we could watch them crash and burn. The Chief looked like he took his model airplane building a little more seriously than that.

A ceiling fan above us rotated slowly.

Finally he set down his model and his tiny brush and stared at me as though I were an unfamiliar strain of something.

"Why'd you do it?"

"Do what?" I asked, hoping the smell of the model's fresh paint was covering up my vodka laden breath.

"You were the first to jump that barricade," The Chief said. "Harold told me you came running over like some crazed animal."

Crazed animal? I almost smiled. It's not every day one's referred to in such terms. I decided to come clean.

"I did it because I'm a fraud," I blurted.

He leaned back, cocked his head. "Excuse me?" he said.

"Look," I sighed. "The only reason I came out here this weekend was for the sheer hell of it. Well, that and to get laid. But now through some strange turn of events I'm a YouTube sensation and I'm also married to a woman I barely know."

"Where are you from, young man?"

"L.A."

He whistled. "That explains some things."

He lit a cigarette and offered me one. Though I'd quit smoking four months ago, this seemed like a good a time as any to pick up the habit again. "Now you say you're a fraud," he said, giving me a light. "What's that mean?"

"It means not only am I not gay, but I'm against the damn war." I said. "I don't think we should be sending anyone over to that hellhole."

The Chief nodded slowly. "I served two tours in 'Nam," he said quietly.

Oh Lord, I thought, here we go.

"Would you have opposed that war?" he asked me.

He might as well have drawn his gun and aimed it at me. Did he think I was a fool? If I said *oh no, sir,* I would obviously be a blatant liar. A President in way over his head has us charge into a foreign country, cause chaos, and then leave the mess for someone else to clean up? Iraq was my generation's Vietnam. But if I said *yes, I would've opposed Vietnam,* well…

The whisk of the ceiling fan above seemed to grow louder as the silence lingered.

I decided I was buzzed enough to be honest and let the chips fall where they may. "No offense meant, sir." I said. "But I imagine so."

Now the sound of the ceiling fan's motion was toppled by The Chief tapping his fingers against his desk and my heart pounding. The edges of the Chief's lips crimped up a bit. "Yeah," he said. "I wasn't all too thrilled with it myself. But I was drafted and I was proud to be a soldier."

"Sir, I respect that." I said earnestly. "I'm not bullshitting you. I respect you and every man and woman who's ever served this country. And I'm not just saying that to-"

"My son," he cut me off. "My son is… he was a… a homosexual. Wanted to serve this country more than anything. Like his dad. But he couldn't because he was gay."

Was? Had this man converted his son to heterosexuality through stringent lessons? Or had he used guilt? Torture?

The Chief wasn't saying anything more, and even though I didn't want to prod him my curiosity got the better of me. "So did he... change?"

"No," The Chief's eyes closed. "He was killed. He was killed by a coupla gay bashers."

Out of all the many many times I've felt like an asshole in my life, that moment immediately took a place in the top five. "I'm sorry," I managed.

"I still can't pretend to understand why he was how he was," The Chief said. "I did everything..."

There came a shouting from outside the office. Someone was protesting that they had rights.

The Chief picked up his brush and dabbed it at the model plane. "What you did out there today, you came out here, you jumped the barricades. First one to do it. Shit, it means something. Just wanted to let you know that."

"Thank you, sir." I said.

He stood up. "I'll walk you to your cell," he said. "We'll keep you all overnight and you'll be out in the morning."

As he led me out of the office, I scanned the walls for any pictures of the Chief with a younger man, any one who could maybe be his son. I saw none.

Good revolutionists fight at all costs

Bad revolutionists sometimes feel lost

The jail cell was cold, and had the usual thin hard "mattresses" and the usual pointless empty feeling. After the Chief dropped me off and I was locked inside, I kept going over the questions I'd wanted to ask: Had they ever caught the murderers? How had he found out his son was gay? What had the Chief meant when he said he'd done everything? Everything right? Everything wrong?

My cellmates, fellow revolutionists, were all gabbing about how wild it was to be in jail. When they saw the Chief escorting me they'd waited until the cell door had closed and he was out of earshot before asking me in excited whispers if that guy had beaten me up or tried to "make me talk."

I didn't answer, just rolled over on my side and mercifully passed out.

Good revolutionists ponder the questions of the deep
Bad revolutionists know when it's time for sleep

True to the Chief's word, after being served a breakfast of milk, microwaved scrambled eggs with biscuits, and a stale Danish, we were released the next morning. No court, no bail, nothing.

We filed out of the cell. Some of the guys were grumbling, saying they wanted to go before a judge because it was bullshit we'd been locked up for a night and they wanted to file official complaints. After all, if we weren't being charged, what crime had we committed?

"Wrong sexuality, wrong time," someone said, and almost everybody laughed. I didn't; I was thinking of the Chief's son. He'd been *killed* for being the wrong sexuality at the wrong time. And these jerks had trespassed on federal property, like me, and they were pissed about a night in jail?

I kept my eyes down as I stepped across the grey tiled floor of the lobby, not wanting to chance the possibility of making eye contact with the Chief. After speaking to him as one human being to another last night, I wanted to preserve that and not have our last contact be captor to prisoner.

Outside there was a small crowd waiting for us. I immediately spotted Carl and Stephanie. When I noted that Stephanie was now sporting a white wedding gown I was almost ready to turn around and bolt back into the safety of the jail.

Before I could do so most of the crowd broke out into applause and a few reporters descended upon me. "You were the one who allegedly 'led the charge' over the barricades yesterday," a woman wearing a crisp blue dress and top dotted with interchanging white triangles shouted at me. "What exactly were you hoping to accomplish?"

When sober, I've never been much good at vocalizing my feelings. Being stone cold sober on a Sunday morning and being asked why I'd done something while half-drunk didn't bode well for me being terribly loquacious.

I almost flipped off this comment, telling the reporter I was just drunk and it seemed like a good idea at the time. But then I thought of the Chief and his son. The Chief trying to understand his son, all of these people who'd marched on the Pentagon, these individuals wanting to come together but not always knowing how best to do so.

"On this Sunday morning," I began. "I can offer you this. I'm not a homosexual. I'm not a Christian. Technically I'm a Jew. I'm a white Jewish male," I added, "And I still can't get one of my screenplays produced in Hollywood."

The reporters, all four of them, matched befuddled frowns. So much for my humor, which also tends to suffer in direct proportion to my sobriety.

"But I'm married to a Christian," I went on quickly. I nodded at Stephanie, who was staring at me wide-eyed. This inspired me. "And Christ taught us to accept one another. In a few weeks this country will see the first African-American sworn into her highest office. It's a testament not only to America, but to human nature, that this historic event will take place.

"That, my friends, is what I was attempting to demonstrate through my actions. As a country, as a people, we must be accepting of one another. It's not about war, it's not about combat… this march, along with my actions, as incomprehensible as they may seem… it's all been about something more." Here I paused. What the hell had it all been about?

"Acceptance." I concluded.

The crowd seemed skeptical. "Can I get an 'amen?'" I shouted.

The few scattered "amens" were far outnumbered by the silent perplexed expressions of those I'd just preached to.

So I wasn't Jim Bakker. To hell with it. I just wanted to get out of there. As I started down the steps the reporters stepped back and gave me a wide berth. I almost laughed as I thought of Moses parting the Red Sea. "Hey, Moses," one of the writers of the Holy Bible probably called out, "You part this shallow sea and I'll guarantee you two paragraphs in the New Testament."

I was immediately ashamed at such blasphemous thoughts. And on a Sunday to boot.

I certainly wasn't Moses, but evidently I was going to get some kind of publicity, even if The *Arlington Gazette* is a far cry from the Holy Bible. But I hoped at least one of the papers would print something close to what I'd said and the Chief might pick up a copy tomorrow and read it and understand.

I caught up with Stephanie and Carl, who were walking away at a quick speed. "Hey guys!" I said. "Where are you going? Were you just gonna leave me here?"

Stephanie turned to face me, tears on her cheeks. "I'm sorry, Shawn!" she said. "We can't be married!"

A reprieve! It was as though I'd just received a governmental pardon of sorts. I tried to make my sigh one of resignation and not relief. "Okay," I said.

"I owe you an explanation," she said.

"No, you really don't." I answered quickly.

"You're Jewish," she said. "My parents would never bless our marriage. They believe that… all Jews are sinners."

"For what, killing Jesus?" I proposed.

"Yes," she said. "And if they knew I'd slept with you…"

She shuddered.

"Well, they don't have to know." I assured her.

I didn't bother to point out that technically I'd been *born* a Jew in accordance with a Jewish law that proclaims if your mother's Jewish, you're Jewish. In actuality, I had about as much choice in the matter as homosexuals did at being born gay. Sure, I could "grapple" with it, the way some high-profile priests "grapple" with their homosexual thoughts. I didn't believe in organized religion, my Hebrew vocabulary consisted pretty much of *Shalom, Mazel Tov, L'Chayim, Lox* and for some reason I've never been able to recall, *Gefilte fish*. Thus I'd never really considered myself Jewish. But at this stage in the game, if it meant not having to marry this woman, I was never more proud to be a Jew and never more grateful for anti-Semitism.

"Tell you what," I smiled. "How about you guys give me a ride to the airport, and we'll just say the marriage is annulled."

They agreed, and on the way to the airport, Carl found a station on satellite radio that was running an ABBA marathon. "Dancing Queen" came on and I began to sing along. Carl joined in and soon Stephanie did as well. By the time we cruised through the streets near the Pentagon (which were surprisingly clean, with not a trace of litter from yesterday's march) all three of us were in harmony. I didn't know what the weekend had proved or meant, if anything, but on this day of rest a gay Christian man, a bisexual Christian woman, and an undecided Jew were united in their love for dancing.

For the moment, that was enough.

Good revolutionists get on the government's blacklist

Bad revolutionists get on the government's do-not-call list

LIVING IN PARADISE

When I first arrived in Southern California, I brought with me several fantasies, one more unorthodox than the next. Becoming a professional wrestler was certainly not a usual goal that so-called normal folks carry with them from the Midwest. Neither, for that matter, is becoming a sky diving instructor or a shark hunter, two other careers I considered potentialities.

There was another dream that burned inside me, one who many seem to share here in L.A. That of becoming a writer, partying and creating the days away in a land where it never snows. Though the details of my projected canon were vague at best, I was certain its tomes would contain vibrant observations and tales that would illustrate people's desire to shatter life's joyous melancholy, how moments worth reliving aren't necessarily always happy ones, how it's possible to experience contradictory emotions in the space of time it takes to complete a sentence, etc.

One of the many obstacles to tackle was I had no idea of any coherent way to address these matters. But I *was* looking forward to my pursuit of them, which would certainly involve wild bouts of drinking and nights of decadence that would then wind themselves into stories that chronicled the ebb and flow of the human condition.

I'd even envisioned the title of my first novel. *A Work In Progress.* How cool would that be, I assumed, to have someone ask another what they were reading and the reply to be, "A work in progress." I beamed with pride at the thought of my first work having as clever a title as Philip Roth's *The Great American Novel.*

Having determined the name of my unwritten first novel and at the same time vaulting myself into the company of a National Book Award winner despite yet writing a word, I settled down to having wild bouts of drinking and nights of decadence. All, I maintained, in the name of research.

Unfortunately, though enjoyable, these episodes neither helped me understand the human condition nor helped me make headway on my immortal novel. All they helped me determine that being a writer would probably be a much more enjoyable gig if it didn't so involve actually sitting down in front of a blank page and *writing.* Perhaps, I reasoned, I wasn't quite ready for such a task.

In the meantime, though, it had become abundantly clear that skydiving instruction and shark hunting were out of the running as far as paths I was qualified to follow. Jumping our of an airplane at thirteen thousand feet was a wonderfully enlightening experience in that it made me aware not only how beautiful the earth can be while soaring down toward it at a daring speed but also that I never wanted to go through that again. It was kind of how I imagined I'd feel about being in a porno movie; it would be fun once but I wouldn't want to do it for a living. As for shark hunting it took me roughly forty-five minutes of scuba diving to realize that I was scared enough of being down that deep in the ocean without the added threat of getting a leg bit off. Jaws could breathe easy. It was apparent I would have to pursue a career that involved a job where my feet could be firmly planted on the ground.

So I switched to yet another backup plan and enrolled in college, where I majored in Radio, Television and Film. This mostly involved watching films, writing essays comparing these various films, directing shorts, and smoking cigarettes outside in the Quad with fellow film students.

Upon the day I graduated college with a Bachelors degree in RTVF with a minor in Screenwriting, I had my tongue firmly in cheek. My plan was to dash off a few spec scripts that would sell for low-to-mid six figures, and then once I'd established a bankroll, settle down to serious work on *A Work In Progress.*

Given my fantastical assumptions, it's possible that alcohol was already beginning to decimate my brain cells at an alarming rate.

A couple years passed while I wrote several scripts, all of which I submitted to agents, and all of which were returned accompanied by polite letters that began with a variation on the theme "After reading your work with great interest, we're sorry to say that

a) we're not taking on new clients at this time
b) your writing isn't compatible with our agency
c) the current economic climate makes it impossible for us to take on such edgy material
d) you suck

I proudly tacked these missives to a bulletin board, chortling to myself how I'd one day be able to use this as a colorful anecdote when reporters asked about my beginning years.

But as these beginning years began creeping up on slightly more middle-aged ones, I began to get nervous. My "wall of rejection" (as I'd christened it what seemed like a lifetime ago), had become so thick with letters it now seemed an impenetrable fortress.

I did have a few things going for me. One was my rumored insanity. Friends were always telling me I was nuts, so I'd gradually accepted this to be true. After all, manic-depression had gripped my mom, her mother, and three of her mother's sisters. I figured why not be the first male in the family to carry on that tradition, which could prove as productive as it could debilitative. Lord Byron, Sylvia Plath, Virginia Woolf, Malcom Lowry, Sinclair Lewis… the list of well known bipolar writers seemed endless. True, many had wound up committing suicide or dying in fits of madness. But as someone who really did long to be a writer who created words that might help make sense of a world that often seemed to have gone mad itself, I figured if a tragic end was the price to pay then so be it. Besides, I'd long ago dismissed the suggestion that I take lithium or other assorted medications once I learned you couldn't drink while on them.

Which brought me to my second secret weapon for success as a writer: alcoholism. Whenever I picked up the biographies of famous writers, I immediately looked at the index and was always reassured at how many pages *alcoholism of* dealt with.

It was a wonderful conundrum. Which came first, the bipolar rollercoaster of mania and depression, or the alcoholism? Did I drink to control my insanity or was I drinking myself into madness? The chicken and the egg had nothing on the existential war that was waging within me every day. This, I reasoned, was just too good a copy for the universe to ignore. Surely a bipolar alcoholic like me was meant to become an author of *some* stature.

The main flaw in my reasoning - that there were numerous homeless people living on the beach just a few miles from my apartment who were afflicted by both conditions and had never published or produced a thing - I ignored.

Meanwhile I was working at a mortgage company as a switchboard operator and on weekends as a phone sex operator. I'd lucked into the phone sex operator position through a friend. The phone sex operator gig was great because, even though it paid a bit less than connecting aspiring and refinancing homeowners to mortgage loan officers, I could go in hammered and still do a great job. My crowning achievement was getting some businessman calling from Baltimore to stand atop his desk in his office, thirty stories up, and fuck himself with a pencil.

Little did I know then, but he probably got off easier than most of the people who were calling the mortgage company to take out loans.

❦ ❦ ❦

It was a hot Southern California day in February when I bought the takeout order of Combination Fried Rice that would change my life.

The meal came with a fortune cookie, and though I'd never been one for fortunes, for some reason I read this one.

You are making progress.

At the mention of a portion of the title of my unfinished novel (after five years I'd managed to complete not only sixteen scripts nobody wanted anything to do with, but 193 grueling pages of *A Work In Progress*), I felt ridiculously inspired. Below my promise of progress were five numbers.

That night I surprised Jake, the clerk at the corner liquor store, by buying a Fantasy Five lottery ticket along with my customary 1.75 liter bottle of vodka. Jake and I had known each other for years and I'd never bought a lottery ticket before.

"What's the occasion?" he asked.

"I'm making progress," I informed him.

The next morning, I logged on to the Internet and checked my numbers. I'd won $214,000.

Progress awaited.

After taxes, I had about $150,000. I quit my two jobs, then announced to my friends that I would finally be able to "hunker down and finish this beast of a novel."

Unfortunately, I was also free to hunker down and make an ass of myself.

Amongst my various groups of friends, I'd always enjoyed a reputation as "the life of the party," "the whip," and "the one most likely to get arrested before the night was over." Now, with money in my pocket, I was more dangerous than ever. Having wealth gave me an illusory feeling of invincibility. At the very least I figured that, outside of murder, I'd be able to afford bail for any drunken shenanigan I might be arrested for.

Though extraordinarily enough I never got arrested, I did manage to savagely alienate all of my friends. Often I heard the stories third hand, being that I was usually in a blackout when they occurred. There was the incident at a friend's wedding reception when, as he and his new bride were performing their slow dance to the tune of "Cheek to Cheek," I strutted onto the dance floor, embraced them both, then pulled my pants down and wiggled my boxers at the astonished guests, boxers which bore the AC/DC song title: DIRTY DEEDS DONE DIRT CHEAP.

Scratch Timmy as a friend.

There was another regrettable occurrence at another party, where I supposedly began kissing a statue of Jesus Christ full on the lips while murmuring, "Come back, baby." That this happened at the home of a friend whose wife was a born-again Christian didn't help matters, and I was asked rather aggressively to vacate their home. A few days later a letter arrived that was signed by both my friend and his wife which informed me they were praying for me to seek help for my addictions that I used to fill the void in my soul. I wrote a letter back saying that that was precisely what I'd been trying to do in seeking help from their statue of Christ. *Hellfire and brimstone,* I phrased (I thought cleverly) *who* isn't *waiting for the second coming?*

When I got no response, I checked another friend off the list.

There was the night I supposedly screamed at people while riding shotgun in a friend's convertible down Sunset Boulevard, calling them bourgeois pigs. Or the time I'd been wearing my leather pants and had been so drunk that when we stopped off at Pink's Hot Dog Stand after a night of carousing I fell and spilt my pants open down the middle, my testicles hanging out of the tear. My friends ushered me out to the patio and left me alone for thirty seconds, which proved to be a mistake. Somehow in my drunken haze I recognized Martin Landau sitting at a table in the corner, trying to enjoy a chili cheese dog in peace. I stood and approached him, bellowing *"Bel-a!"* in reference to the legendary actor he'd so expertly portrayed in the movie *Ed Wood.* I dimly recall his look of horror as I spilled the combo #4 (Polish sausage and turkey burger with chili) I'd forgotten I was holding all over his overcoat before my buddies were able to wrest me away and stuff me into the car.

Friends reacted to these incidents with amusement that climbed up to alarm and finally graduated to disgust. People began to drift away, getting married and sturdily ascending the ladder of their respective professions. I had no such aspirations. I was content to live what I generously termed "the simple life," which meant that if I banged out four or five pages of my novel, made it to the gym, and by four in the afternoon was already working on a good buzz, the day was a success.

There were still women in my life. However, I managed to mangle these relationships as well, being that I had as much trouble settling down with one woman as America does settling down with a partner in the Middle East. I sure as hell hadn't found my Israel. As a result, there was frequent turmoil. Though the studio apartment I lived in was inside a gated complex, I made the mistake of giving out the gate code to various ladies I happened to be seeing at the same time.

This led to several unfortunate skirmishes, none of which ended particularly well. The final one involved a frustrated actress showing up at my door at 2:30 in the morning, pounding on it and crying that she was going to kill herself. I was in bed with a screenwriter who, earlier in the evening while we'd been bar hopping, had also promised she was going to commit suicide that night as soon as I fell asleep and – her words – "give me something to write about." I hadn't slept a wink and was wide awake when the actress began pounding on the door. I had the brilliant thought to introduce the suicidal actress outside my door to the suicidal screenwriter in my bed. At the very least they'd have something in common.

I'd been drinking that night and it's possible my reasoning was clouded.

As I rolled out of bed and went to open the door, I thought of a passage in Janet

Fitch's *White Oleander.* The main character had fantasized at one point bout how alluring it might be to be the kind of person who would orchestrate multiple lovers at a time. The book had been an Oprah's Book Club choice, and for good reason; it was a brilliant work. But as I opened the door, I wondered if perhaps the potentialities of reality were not all that the protagonists of fiction cracked them up to be.

The suicidal actress threw her arms around me. "I need to talk to you!" she cried. "I'm so..."

A pause. I felt her shift her body in order to peer around me. "Who's in your bed?" she demanded.

"Who the hell is that?" the screenwriter shrieked from behind.

While I stood there, helpless to do anything but breathe and see what happened next, the actress shoved me aside as the screenwriter leapt up from bed.

"I need to talk to my man!" the actress shouted. "So get out of here!"

"He's my man!" the screenwriter shouted back.

I chose this cue to duck into the kitchen and hurriedly open the freezer. I didn't bother mixing a drink, just took a shot straight from the bottle. I crept back to the living room/bedroom area as their voices grew louder in volume.

"You don't mean anything to him!" the actress was yelling at the screenwriter.

"Oh, and I suppose you think you do?" the screenwriter shot back.

"Stop!" I urged them, as quietly as possible, being that it was 2:30 in the morning and my neighbors had complained numerous times in the past couple months about the fights and the noisy lovemaking sessions coming from my apartment at random hours. "What the hell are you two fighting over me for? I have no car, no real job, and no real prospects! What the hell do you see in me?"

Perhaps it was the genuine curiosity in my voice that halted them so abruptly. They both faced me, and a lengthy silence followed. With every passing second I hoped one of them would blurt out: "But you're a brilliant writer," or "You're the most understanding man I've ever met."

After what seemed like a month of silence I would've settled for, "You put the toilet seat down."

Finally the actress spoke. "I want to save you! You're better than all this," she gestured around at my apartment, at the scattered piles of books, papers, pictures, and bills that spilled over my desk and table and onto the carpet I'd last vacuumed about two years ago. At the parking meter a friend of mine and I had pulled out of the sidewalk one drunken Saturday night that was now leaning against my living room wall. At the poster of Richard Nixon with a motto below that had once read DON'T BE A DICK until I'd strategically blocked out letters so it now read DO A DICK.

The actress turned to the screenwriter. "Isn't he?" she asked.

The screenwriter shrugged.

It occurred to me that both of them seemed to be realizing this was not how thirtysomethings were supposed to live. The characters in the 1980s television show *Thirtysomething* wouldn't have been caught dead in the squalor that served as my natural habitat.

"I'm not sure," the screenwriter said slowly. "Any guy who gives out his security code to more than one person is kind of…"

"Sneaky," the actress proposed.

"Low-down," the screenwriter agreed.

Now they were both glaring at me. "Ladies…" I began. "I didn't want to disappoint either one of you—"

"My God, you've got a bottle in your hand! Always with your drinking!" "Christ, I've tried so hard to understand you, but there's just nothing more I can do!"

By now they'd both kind of blurred into one, so I was unable to determine exactly which of them was saying what. I closed my eyes, hoping when I opened

them I wouldn't see anyone in my apartment other than my stuffed animal Schmoo-
Schmoo.

Then I felt the bottle of vodka being
tugged from my grasp.

My eyes popped open. "Hey, what the
hell-" I yanked the bottle back and held
it to my chest.

"You just stay here and get drunk! I
never want to see you again!" "That goes
for me too!"

The two formerly suicidal women made
their exit, but not before one of them
gave me a shove and the other lashed out
with a left cross that smacked against
the side of my head. I staggered back and
tripped, falling into my rocking chair
while taking care not to drop my precious
cargo.

As soon as the door slammed shut behind
them, I quickly got up and locked the
door. Then I took a contemplative sip of
vodka and vowed for what must have been
the eight hundredth time in my life to
commit myself to celibacy.

In the morning, I settled on asking
the manager if he could please change
the building's security code, the reason being that my wallet had recently
been stolen and it had contained a slip
of paper with the gate code. As a result
I'd been attacked last night by people
who had used said code to get into the

building. The way the manager cocked his
eyebrow told me he wasn't buying this at
all. But he wound up changing the code.

There I was, insulated from the outside
world, independently wealthy, utterly
alone, and free to scribble furiously
day after day on a manifesto that I was
hoping would change how people thought.

Some would call it the recipe for a
serial killer. I called it living in paradise.

THE POET IN THE ELEVATOR

At age 33, I find myself blessed and cursed with a bizarre contentment.

I've managed to finish my immortal novel, but after several dozen rejection letters I've changed the title from *A Work In Progress* to *Wake Up, Asshole!* I feel this new title lends the book an edginess that was lacking before.

Another difference is that now instead of letters, I send out query emails to agents, and instead of pieces of paper rejecting me, I get emails rejecting me. I delete these email rejections immediately, a far cry from back in my confident young years when I'd pinned letters, hundreds of them, to the bulletin board that served as my wall of rejection. The wall of rejection is history by this point. Unable to stand the sight of it any longer, I took the damned thing out into the desert and burned it months ago.

My days have taken on a familiar pattern both reassuring and disturbing, with disturbing getting the edge. I start out with a cocktail at six thirty in the morning, when I rise to check my investments. This cocktail serves to (I tell myself) "greet the inexhaustible capacities for creativity that lurk behind any given hour of any given day."

Whatever the hell that means.

Throughout the morning I write on and off, pour a drink or three, grab breakfast, then head off to the gym.

Back home I stare at the blank screen and run my fingers over the keyboard as though it were a hopelessly limp prick or eternally dry vagina.

Self-doubt is a constant companion. As of late I've begun to fathom the horror of it being entirely possible that although I have a great passion for writing, I'm at the same time completely devoid of talent. Where the hell that leaves me, I don't know. In spite of the economy tanking, I have enough money left over from my lottery win to live on for quite a while, being that I pretty much only spend it on rent, food, vodka, and typing paper. One thing about living alone with no spouse, no kids, and no friends: it helps cut down expenses.

Talking to myself has grown more and more natural, even though the stories I regale myself with and the fights I have with myself are often the same ones over and over. I feel like there's an old married couple hiding out inside my brain, and sometimes I contemplate if this is how people go senile. Gay marriage, the state of pop culture, stem cell research, abortion… I argue with myself about these and other topics in exchanges that often climax into shouting matches. One Thursday afternoon after a particularly heated spat with myself regarding exactly what age the legal drinking age should be lowered to (the radical side of me demanded fourteen while my more rational side proposed seventeen), the apartment manager knocks on my door and tells me one of the neighbors just reported yells coming through the wall. I apologize and explain that I was simply going over dialogue for a scene I'd just written, taking the role of a crazy writer who was going even crazier. Which, I realize as the manager gives a hesitant nod, is more or less true. I am now indisputably one of the things, low on the list as it may have been, I came out to L.A. to become: a writer partying and creating the days away in a land where it never snows.

I'm still writing every day, but have recently decided to resort to poetry. In spite of my assertion to a friend years ago that poetry was for "writers who don't have balls enough to write a novel," with *Wake Up, Asshole!* having been rejected by sixty-three agents so far, I've readjusted my thinking. Poetry, I've determined, is more subtle, written by sensitive souls who don't care about things such as bestseller lists, publishing contracts, or that circulation of their work will likely never eclipse two hundred "special editions." Besides this, writing poetry enables me to submit to an annual "Young Poets Contest" offered by a very prestigious Ivy League school. The reward is a published book, and the only requirements for consideration are that you be under forty years of age, have no more than one hundred and twenty pages worth of poems, and have the $30.00 entry fee. Being just thirty-three years old, I figure that I've got at least six years to become published as a "young poet" before total midlife crisis kicks in.

I enjoy taking walks at night through my neighborhood, and sometimes pick up a copy of U.C.L.A.'s newspaper, the *Daily Bruin.* I tell myself it's to "see what the kids are up to" but I also wonder if it's not me yearning to travel back to my college years, when I hadn't yet learned how easily dreams can splinter when pressed against too much passing time.

One spring evening I settle down with a copy of the *Bruin* and see a notice in the classifieds advertising for temp workers. A company called Health Center Relocations is offering sixteen dollars an hour for people to help move the

U.C.L.A. Medical Center from an older outdated location to a newer facility down the street named after yet another accomplished actor who'd found even more fame in politics.

I haven't set foot in a hospital in at least a decade. I haven't even gone to a doctor for a checkup in years. My political reason is because I don't have proper health coverage, but in truth it's probably because I'd prefer not to be told that my liver is most likely the size of a watermelon.

However, helping move a medical center conjures up the promise of positive karma, and after my dealings with people during my time spent in L.A., I figure I can use all the good karma I can lay my hands on.

So I fabricate a resume, exaggerating the time I worked at a tree removal company from two weeks to two years. Also, I conjure up periods in which I've labored for a moving company, as well as a storage firm. Looking at the resume before I email it I chuckle and tell myself, "Michals, you are so full of shit."

I email it off, then have a half hour argument with myself about how if the President of the United States could falsely claim there were weapons of mass destruction in Iraq, I'm entitled to fudge my employment history.

"But he was the President," I tell myself. "You're just a citizen."

"You're damn right I'm a citizen!" I rage back. "And I have just as much right to lie as those fat cats in Washington do!"

I decide to settle the argument with myself over a drink. God forbid the manager come knocking on my door again. Who knows? The next time could be the last, the one in which he's accompanied by those nice people in white coats, the kind who want you to come along with them "for a quiet chat."

An hour later I'm still mercifully alone with my drink and no knocks at the door, when I get an emailed response that I should be at the loading docks of the new U.C.L.A. Medical Center at seven the next morning.

A few others are already milling about on the loading dock when I arrive. I exchange quick nods with my fellow applicants as we wait. A few guys in their early 20s obviously know each other. I eavesdrop on snatches of their conversation. "so wasted… fell into the bushes… boxers on his head."

Ah, memories.

I'm a little surprised to see that a couple of the assembled appear to be pushing fifty. Soft bodied and balding, these men appear to be the kind of people who have absolutely no business reading a college newspaper. I tell myself that I, being still in my thirties, have every right to read a college newspaper.

Soon a bulky man with a moustache appears and barks out, "You all here for Health Center Relocations, eh?" Before anyone can answer he waves us on, "Then follow me!"

We're led into a small room. Bare hospital beds are piled high and mattresses are stacked against the wall. "My name's Hank, but call me Milt," this man tells us. "What we have here is a serious undertaking. H.C.R. has been contracted for the next two weeks to move the third ranked medical center on this planet. Now our company, though based in Canada, has worked all over the world. We usually work for the U.S. government moving army hospitals, but U.C.L.A. requested us specifically for this move. Two years of preparation have gone into this. The lives of patients are going to be in your hands. So… any of you feel you can't handle it, best leave now."

A blanket of fidgety quiet lay over the room. I think of all the weddings I've been to, when the assembled are requested to speak now or forever hold their peace regarding the impending union.

Milt raises one of his eyebrows, a talent that has always impressed me. "So you all think you're ready to do this, eh? No problem. Just to let you know, some of you won't make it past the first couple days. We tend to weed out the plugs pretty quick."

The rest of the day is spent training, in which we are introduced to gondolas, which are basically bookcases on wheels. Milt explains to us the concept of a human chain, wherein we all line up and push the gondolas and other dollies to one another. "Like a giant ant farm," he proclaims. "And remember, I'm watching you. If you do well, there'll be some bonuses in it for you. If not…"

He gives a nearby post a swift kick. "Out on your ass," he says.

Towards the end of our orientation, he passes around release forms, where we agree to not hold Health Center Relocations or U.C.L.A. responsible for any injuries we may experience on the job.

One man, obviously about thirty or so years removed from college, raises a pudgy arm. "Pardon me, um, but how would we get injured on this job?"

Milt smiles and raises his left pants leg. A scar so pronounced it looks like a thin bubble decorates his calf.

"Got this in Germany," he says, unmistakable pride in his voice. "The edge of a bed gashed my calf. Took forty stitches. Good news is, if you get injured on

this job, you're already at a hospital. They'll fix you up right away. Now
I'll see you all here tomorrow at seven
o'clock sharp!"

The next day, the man who asked the
question about possibly getting injured
on the job doesn't show.

"One plug down, eh." Milt drawls, nodding at the rest of us.

The first day turns out to be fairly
slow. Only one truck comes in and we
unload it within twenty minutes. The rest
of the day we lounge around like those
Mafioso characters in movies who play
cards at construction sites and get paid
good money to do so. The most exciting
thing that happens that day is two of
the frat guys almost get into a fistfight
over whether Kobe Bryant is the greatest basketball player ever. Right before
it looks like they're about to come to
blows, I laugh out loud.

Both stop and focus on me.

"No offense intended, guys." I say
quickly. *Terrific, Michals. First day on
the job and you're already making friends
and influencing people.* "It's just that
Kobe Bryant's a multi-millionaire who
doesn't even know you two… or *any* of us
for that matter…" I gesture around, hoping that the inclusion of our coworkers
will somehow unite us as one. "He doesn't

even know we're alive. Why do you care so much about him?"

They regard me carefully, then kind of glance at each other. I try to maintain a rugged thoughtful pose.

Then they turn back to me and shrug. "Just because," one of them, a guy I've heard addressed as D-Man by his frat brothers, replies.

"Works for me," I shrug back. "Well, carry on then."

Both D-Man and his buddy start to crack up, shaking their heads as though they've just stumbled upon some form of foreign being. Behind me I hear someone murmur, "that dude seems a little cracked."

Well, I think. Didn't take long for *that* to come to light.

Later that afternoon Milt calls me over. "Shawn, you're gonna be our elevator guy."

"Okay," I say hesitantly.

"What does this mean? It means that you need to stand guard by one of the elevators. When the cargo comes in, you're going to be in charge of transporting it to the proper floor. This position of responsibility makes you the most important link in our human chain, so you need to be on your toes, eh?"

I'm intrigued, if not outright stunned. It's been a while since someone's entrusted me with responsibility of *any* kind.

"I'm curious... why me?" I ask. "I mean don't get me wrong, I'm happy to do it. Proud to do it." I add. "But why me?"

"Well, you showed a clear head today when you defused that Kobe Bryant debate." Milt replies. "I don't see why the hell anyone should care about him either. Couldn't hold a candle to Doctor J or Larry Bird."

He peers at me as though he expects me to be intimately familiar with these names, so I give a definitive nod.

"These kids today..." he shakes his head. "By the way," he asked. "How old are you? About forty?"

"Forty just last month," I lie in confirmation. It's the first time in more than a decade, when I was trying to buy beer while underage, that I've actually exaggerated my age.

Milt nods. "Look pretty damn good for your age."

"Clean living," I smile.

Day three. I've been standing post for hours at an elevator reserved strictly for Health Center Relocations, and only three truckloads have come in all day. Since I've started writing poetry, I like to believe that if one is armed with poetry or creativity, one is immune to boredom. However, by 3:13 in the afternoon I not only know how many cracks there are in each individual tile within a six foot radius, but am willing to admit that there are only so many times a day one can mentally recite Rudyard Kipling's *If* and still get a tingling in their toes.

On the plus side, I've been given a walkie-talkie so that I can coordinate with the various Collared Guys on the different floors for pick-ups and deliveries. Collared Guys are the company's full time employees, our superiors, and wear white collared shirts with "HCR" stamped in large bold letters across the chest. We temps have been issued blue t-shirts with HCR stamped in small letters above the heart.

Today Milt asks me what it is I do. "I mean, you're a little old to still be in college," he begins.

"I'm a writer," I answer quickly. This is true enough, but then comes the inevitable follow-up question: what have I written?

Numerous screenplays that have never been produced, a novel that I can't seem to find an agent for, and dozens of poems in preparation for the "Young Poets Contest."

This is the painful, truthful answer. But I find myself articulating a quite different, much more forgiving set of facts. According to what I'm saying I've worked as an uncredited writer on several projects for major studios and have assisted as a ghostwriter for the autobiographies of numerous professional wrestlers. I also have not one but two novels with a New York agent and, as they say in the industry, "deals are pending."

Milt whistles. "Wow. What the heck are you doing here, eh?"

"I often take temp jobs like this, you know, to get material."

All the guys wearing collars have nicknames. Reach, Jenkins, Winston, Sherlock, etc. Hank's nickname, Milt, comes from the movie classic *Bachelor Party,* which starred a young Tom Hanks. In the movie, Milt is the name of a pimp's enforcer. When I ask him how he came to be christened with this particular nickname, he only smiles. "Just don't screw up and you won't find out," he says.

By the fifth day I've begun to get to know my fellow temps. There's D-Man and Jamster, the two guys who were ready to brawl with each other over Kobe Bryant's status as the greatest basketball player ever. They belong to a fraternity named Delta Delta Tau, and their dedication to professional sports borders on the fanatic, turn out to be interesting and intelligent people. Jamster maintains a constant monologue that incorporates the rise and fall of Irish poets such as Dylan Thomas with the rise and fall of the Los Angeles Lakers this season. D-Man is the more silent of the two, and always seems as though he's staring at a horizon, even if he's just looking across the loading docks.

Joseph is a young man whose family emigrated from Israel. He's impeccably polite, always referring to everyone as "sir." Trevor has tattoos and long hair. He's a musician, and can usually be found grinning and tapping an imaginary set of drums. There's only one woman. A twenty year old named Beth, who has been christened Weez for reasons that never become readily apparent.

Then, sometimes the best nicknames are those that remain shrouded in mystery.

One afternoon near the end of our first week, Joseph asks me, "Sir, I'm curious. Why do you like writing so much?"

Lately I've been asking myself the same question. The curious thing is though I love to write, I don't always particularly *like* it all that much. Sitting down before a blank space that just *smiles* at you as if secure in its own blankness and daring you to try and fill it, doesn't always inspire fond thoughts. There were many days when, after staring at an empty computer screen for hours, I would welcome the delivery of the mail just so I could tear up brochures and other assorted flyers that, though of no enduring literary value, someone had actually managed to fill with pictures and writing. My jealous rage satisfied, I would sit back down to the computer, pleased that I hadn't seen fit to harm a blank piece of paper.

What could I tell Joseph? That at this stage of my life, writing seems to have edged its way into my heart. It's like when parents say of their offspring, "I love (insert name), but I don't *like* him." Writing has, for better or worse, become a part of me.

However, right now I'm too embarrassed to reveal such a fact to people I've known for less than a week. Fortunately, I'm armed with several stock answers I've always pictured myself proposing to imaginary future interviewers whenever queried as to why I write so much. "Why do you like breathing so much?" "When I was young something very heavy fell on my head and I haven't been the same since." My personal favorite: "Because when I'm writing I forget how much I can't stand myself."

Everyone is staring at me, awaiting a response. I decide, under the circumstances, to go for the breathing explanation.

It gets the laugh I've often fantasized about from a studio audience. From all except Joseph, who seems to actually ponder my response before explaining: "I *don't* always like breathing that much. That is to say, I mean… life can be kind of depressing at times. I really am curious. What makes you want to be a writer?"

Grasping at straws, I say, "It's a way of transportation. Like what we're doing here. Each of us has our roles to play. Some unload the trucks, others form the chain along the hallways, and a few of us run the elevators to get things to where they need to go. We're all links. In that, we're all like words. Words link and form a sentence. Sentences form ideas. What are we all but a band of ideas coming together, sometimes in line, sometimes contradictory… but always growing… going places we don't always want to go? Writers help us move from one place to the other."

I'm rambling at this point, and I tell myself as much. "Stop it, Shawn. You're rambling," I say to myself.

Odd looks are coming at me from all around. From the curious manner in which not only my fellow grunts but also all the Collared Guys are staring at me, I get the feeling that today may wind up being my last day on the job. Fine, I figure, I'll go home and sit in my apartment and stare at the walls and wonder what it all means.

Then Joseph pipes up, "That sir, is a bit of poetry."

His words split the confusion. Suddenly everyone's laughing.

From that day forward I have a nickname. Poet.

It's mysterious enough for me.

As the second week progresses we begin to become inundated by a steady stream of trucks, all jammed with supplies, furniture, and equipment from the old hospital. We're responsible for moving everything from hospital beds to office furniture to x-ray machines. Late one afternoon Milt casually informs me that we probably moved about two million dollars worth of machinery that day.

"Ultrasounds," he says. "EKG machines, and that big hairy mother - that's what anesthesiologists use to measure the dosages to put people under for surgery. Good thing we didn't drop it, eh?"

An odd thing happens. That night, sitting in my rocking chair with a book in one hand and a cocktail in the other, I'm attacked by a sense of responsibility for not only my life, but for others as well. I realize with more than a bit of alarm that my existence may actually have an impact on the lives of the hundreds of patients we're going to be moving from one hospital to another in a week's time.

The next morning, I forgo the eye opener I usually have before heading into work.

That afternoon, four truckloads come in at once. I'm on fire, barking commands into my walkie-talkie ("Four gs and six reds to floor eight!"), loading the elevators to capacity. I feel capable, fired up, caught up in the idea that I'm making a difference of some kind. It's the first time in a long while I've ever experienced such passion about anything other than writing.

The next day Trevor tells me, "Hey Poet, I'm having a party Saturday night. You coming?"

At first I think he's joking; a party with a pack of college kids? Surely I'm too old for that kind of thing. But then flashes of *National Lampoon's Animal House* come back to me. Teachers getting stoned with their students. Dean's wives having drunken sex with students. If older people could party with college students back in the 1970s, why not keep that tradition going in the 21st Century?

"Are you serious?" I ask him.

"Hell yeah!" he claps me on the back. "Something tells me you're hilarious when you're drunk."

He has no idea.

That Saturday night, when I walk inside the cramped apartment in a building situated on one of the hilly avenues that surround U.C.L.A., I take one look around the room at all these people who have just recently passed drinking age and wonder what the hell I'm doing there. These young men and women have probably never felt their knees crack, never worried about having that extra green chili burrito at midnight for fear of what their stomach may do to them the next day, and never cast suspicious glances at a peculiar dark lump on their rear right shoulder that seems to be growing year by year.

Just as I'm ready to retreat, telling myself that I really shouldn't miss The Rolling Stones as musical guests on tonight's *Saturday Night Live* (even though I don't own a television), Trevor spots me and swoops over. He introduces me around as "Shawn. But we call him Poet."

A girl in a Hello Kitty dress approaches. She's short, exotic looking, and has a smattering of freckles. "Wow, are you really a poet?" her voice boasts an accent somewhere in the European Union.

I assure her I am. A published poet, in fact, not mentioning that my only recently "published" poem has simply been one posted just the past month on a blog site entitled: "AM I BIPOLAR OR JUST EXTREMELY NORMAL?"

"That is so cool!" she says, leaning into me a bit. She smells like peppermint. "I'm Traci."

She goes on to tell me that she loves to party, try new things, and is "in total awe of poets and people who are open minded."

"Is that vodka?" she asks me, noting the bottle in my hand.

I nod.

"I love vodka," she smiles. "The only thing is it makes me totally horny."

I wonder amazedly where women like this were back in *my* college years. That evil period of the nineties, when darkness reigned across the partying landscape and it was all about grunge, depression and horrible looking clothes.

Times, obviously, have changed. I hold up the bottle of vodka. "In that case," I say. "Bottoms up, Traci."

As I pour us drinks, she asks, "By the way, how old are you?"

"Twenty-six," I lie, subtracting seven years this time instead of adding them like I did with Milt.

"Cool," Traci giggles. "I like older guys."

The party spins wonderfully out of control. Soon I'm dancing with Traci on the patio and taking my turn at beer pong when required. For those of you unfamiliar with the rules of beer pong, ask someone who knows, because by this time I was too drunk to fully comprehend the game. Something about throwing ping-pong balls into opposing teams' cups full of beer, drinking and gradually getting too wasted to form a coherent sentence.

I blame beer pong for what happened next.

By this time Traci and I are groping each other wildly and I'm wishing I could transport myself back in time, back when I'd actually been a reasonable age to be at this party. Then again, back then I would've been too shy to even talk to this woman, so I decide to roll with the changes and kiss her deeply while her hands roam dangerously close to my crotch.

Then I'm called on to make a final shot in the beer pong game. Instead of chancing a throw from across the table, I take a running dive and as the table collapses beneath me I manage to slam the ping-pong ball into the final cup of our opponents.

Doused in beer, it's decided that I should become an honorary member of Delta Delta Tau. Evidently I've passed a test of some sort. Traci has disappeared somewhere, but I'm too preoccupied with my current quest to be concerned. I accompany D-Man, Jamster, and a few others down the street to the Delta Delta Tau house, where I'm led into a room and asked to put on a fur hat with two horns sticking out of its sides, leather shoulder pads lined with spikes, and a pink strap-on dildo.

"You've gotta be kidding me," I slur.

After a few more beers I gradually don this ensemble, and am then led in a chant along the lines of "humping, pumping, sixty-nining chicks, workin' it to the limit with the fattest baddest dicks. Rockin' sockin' whatcha gonna do, when the bros of DDT run wild on *you?!*"

Later I was to learn that no one has ever undergone this sacred initiation ceremony while sober.

That night ends with me waking up in the gutter, literally, at the corner of Wilshire and Westwood Boulevard.

I look around and across the street, displayed on a bank clock's face, is the current time: *4:19.* Judging from the surrounding darkness and chill in the air, I assume it's in the A.M.

"Hey, buddy!"

I turn. Here's a guy with wild red hair running down to his back. His flesh is grizzled and his eyes are slits. He's easily at least fifty years old.

I push myself up from the curb to a half-standing, half-staggering position. "Look man," I say. "I don't have any—"

"Want some?" he asks, and thrusts something out at me.

I jump back, expecting a knife. But when I manage to focus I see he's holding a jar of peanuts. He shakes them lightly.

"Been on the road you're on myself," he drawls. "Nothing like a couple peanuts to give you fuel."

I recoil, offended and fearful that this homeless being who reeks of years spent wandering sees himself fit to tell me what road I'm on.

Then I look down at the peanuts he's offering and realize how hungry I am. I help myself to a small handful, and the person before me laughs. "Take some more, brother," he says.

I do so. "Thanks," I tell him.

He waves and drifts off down the street.

While munching the peanuts I look either way down Wilshire Boulevard for a bus. I'm pretty sure there's a Metro that runs twenty-four hours, but it only comes by once an hour this early in the morning. After trying to flag down a few cabs and being ignored, I walk out in the middle of the street and stand in front of an oncoming one. It screeches to a halt and I zip around and hop in the back.

The cabby seems frightened and starts to explain in broken English that he's on his way to pick someone up—

I thrust a twenty at him and say, "Take me home and keep the change."

I give him my address and once he real-
izes that I'm not a carjacker but simply
a groggy victim of too much fun who's
going to pay him twenty bucks for a ten
dollar ride, he agrees.

I settle back in my seat and look out
the rear window, still picking peanuts
from my palm and eating them one by one.
My homeless friend is walking back in the
same direction of the cab, but after we
pass the corner of Veteran Avenue, the
buildings' shadows have swallowed him up.

That Monday morning, my coworkers
break into cheers when I show up at the
loading dock. "Thought you were a goner
on Saturday night, Poet!" D-Man calls
out to me as I climb the steps to the
loading dock.

"Not me!" I bellow in my best frater-
nal tone while giving him a high-five.

Jamster inquires as to where exactly I
disappeared. Apparently after I was ini-
tiated into Delta Delta Tau, we'd gone to
a college bar, where I'd last been spotted making out with a blonde woman before
vanishing.

"Did you go home with her or what?"
D-Man asks with a wink.

What can I tell them? That not only do
I not have a clue, but that I woke up on
Wilshire Boulevard in the gutter beside
a homeless drifter who'd identified me as

one of his own and was kind enough to share his peanuts with me?

Being an alleged writer, I feel it's my duty to spice reality up a bit. I tell my rapt listeners (temps and Collared Guys both) a story about the black lights in the mystery blonde's apartment that made the glitter she spread across her naked body glow like stars in the sky. About the cat o' nine tails she requested I use on her. And the flavored lubricants. And the edible underwear—

"Sir," Joseph interrupts me. "Are you making this up?"

"Why would you ask that?" I ask sharply.

"Because I think I know her," he replies. "She was in one of my Accounting classes last spring. And she just didn't… well, she didn't look the type."

My heart's pounding. I'm certain I'm about to break out into a cold sweat and reveal that most of my life has often felt like a carefully enhanced creation, so why should this night have been any different. Instead I manage to say, "Looks can be deceiving, young Jedi." And everyone hoots and hollers and claps me on the back. Everyone, that is, but Joseph. My lone story critic just keeps staring at me with an indifferent look on his face.

Throughout the week, we are constantly reminded that Moving Day is coming on

Sunday. This will be the day when we are
responsible for moving over four hundred patients, some of whom are dying,
some of whom have just given birth, and
several of whom are crazy. They will all
share one common suit; they're too frag-
ile to be discharged, and thus it's our
duty to make sure they safely make it the
half mile from the old hospital to their
new medically advanced home, which will
promise better views as well as superior
structural protection against earth-
quakes.

Horror stories abound from past Moving Days. Milt relates his favorite Moving Day tale on Thursday afternoon while
we're in the elevator taking a load of
four Gs and five reds up to floor number
seven.

"It was in Canada. A smaller hospital
was being absorbed into a bigger hospital
that had just been built next to it. The
small hospital was a mental hospital, eh?
So we had to shuttle all these loo-loos
through this flannel tunnel we got set up.
I get this one character, he's in chains,
he's got four armed guards around him, and
we're walking through the tunnel when he
starts talking to himself about how the
birds and the bees are particularly loud
today. He starts asking himself which
ones are louder, then starts yelling at
himself. 'The birds are louder,' 'No, the

bees are louder!' Anyway, we get to the elevator and there's only enough room for me, him, and just one guard. We're on our way up and he's practically foaming at the mouth when he turns to *me* and asks which are louder, the birds or the bees. What the hell am I supposed to say, eh? He looks like he's gonna go for my jugular if I give the wrong answer. I manage to stall until we reach the floor. Then as this joker's being led out, I decide what the hell, it's been a long elevator ride and I deserve a little fun. 'Neither,' I call out to him. He screams, 'Bullshit!' and tries to get back onto the elevator, but the doors close in time."

"Wow," I say, a bit shaken, but only because the idea of someone who argues with themselves strikes me as more of a kindred spirit than a potential murderer. "Did you ever find out what he did?"

Milt grunts. "That's the kinda funny part. One of the doctors said the guy just showed up there at the hospital one day, demanding to be institutionalized, eh. They'd never been able to ascertain his identity. Supposedly this guy usually behaved pretty mellow. Apparently he'd demanded to be put in manacles and surrounded by armed guards that day because he thought the media was gonna be there, and he wanted to appear dangerous. Can you imagine?"

I don't answer. I'm too preoccupied imagining myself being escorted in manacles and surrounded by armed guards. The image looks pretty cool. It imparts a certain aura of danger, and after all, who doesn't like to be thought of as more dangerous than they actually are?

"What the heck's so funny, eh?" Milt asks.

I stop chuckling. "Nothing," I say.

When the elevator doors open, he gets out a little more quickly than usual.

That day another incident occurs which will cause people to question my sanity, or lack thereof. I'm standing guard at the elevator about three in the afternoon, when a lot of the maintenance staff gets off work. I welcome them onto the elevator. They're all Hispanic women, save for one stocky guy who's been taken on by the hospital via a social rehabilitation program for former gang members.

As they crowd into the elevator, a doctor comes rushing up, saying, "I need to get to the eighth floor. Stat!"

I've learned a few code words in my ten days at the new hospital. "Stat" means sooner than already there, which loosely translates to "someone is dying." Although not officially open yet the new facility has begun to take on overflow patients from the old center.

Upon hearing this doctor's request, I immediately press the button for floor eight. But as soon as the doors close, a beefy tattooed arm reaches out from behind me to press the first floor button.

"No!" I shout, and before I can employ any common sense whatsoever I smack the arm away. "This doctor needs to get to a patient. Can't you understand that?"

"Hey man," a deep voice comes from behind, close enough so that I can feel breath on the back of my neck. "We've been working a long day, and we want to go home."

The arm remains in the air beside me. The tattoos are a jumble of skulls and gothic lettering and other symbols I don't want to know the meaning of. We're already passing the fourth floor, so there's no turning back now. Besides I feel compelled by that damned sense of responsibility that's been haunting me the past week or so.

"Listen," I say. "We've all had long days. But I've got a doctor in this elevator, and there's an emergency, and therefore she takes priority. I'm taking her to where she needs to be."

Good Lord, is this really *me* speaking in such a calm confident manner? And to think just four days ago I was waking up in a gutter.

The elevator bell *dings,* and its doors open onto the eighth floor. The doctor hurries out while mouthing a quick "thank you" to me.

Before I gather my senses enough to make a run for it, the doors have closed and we're on our way down. The ladies are talking quietly in Spanish. I catch a few words: *loco, cojones, gringo.* Meanwhile I'm picturing a potential headstone: *Here Lies Shawn Michals… He Lived, He Wrote and Drank, He Died Responsibly.*

Nine of the longest seconds of my life later we arrive at the first floor. When the doors open, my fellow passengers file out without looking at me.

All except one.

I'm taking deep breaths and considering the potential outcomes of a violent assault in a hospital elevator. Milt's first day speech comes back to me. At least if this guy slices me open, I'm in a hospital where they can stitch me back up fairly quickly.

I turn to face him. His dark eyes study me impassively.

"When I got this…" he pulls up his shirt to reveal a scar along his rib cage shaped like a grotesquely exaggerated frown. "After I called 911, we had to wait forty-five minutes for the ambulance. They don't respond that quick in the neighborhood where I used to live."

"I'm sorry," I say, not sure why.

"Nothin' to be sorry about, man. You was just doing your job."

He holds out his hand.

Scared, I still manage to shake it. "See you tomorrow," he says, and leaves.

The next day, the story leaks out when the doctor comes down to personally thank me. "That patient was in kidney failure," she tells me in front of the whole crew on the loading docks. "By standing up to that gangster, you may very well have saved that person's life."

I try to explain that the guy was less a gangster than any driver one might encounter on any given L.A. Freeway at any given afternoon hour. After a day's work, many people tend to become immune to the welfare of others. This guy had been no different; he was just someone who'd been tired and wanted to get home. Inconsiderate, yes, but even though he'd used to in a gang did that automatically make him still a gangster? No. He may as well have been acting like any overworked stockbroker, producer, or personal assistant in this town.

Still, my colleagues urge me to point him out when he walks by. When he does, sometime mid-afternoon, we exchange respectful nods. As soon as he's out of earshot everyone breaks into excited whispers.

"That guy looks hardcore for sure," Jamster determines.

"Did you see those tats?" Trevor asks, as though anyone could've missed them.

Even Weez is staring at me with a distinct shine in her eyes.

Milt beams like a proud papa. "I knew I made a good decision, putting you in charge of the elevator. It's an instinctive gift, don't ask me where I got it."

Joseph sums up the general consensus when he says, "Sir, I admire you for standing up to that guy. But you must be crazy."

Unlike my drunken blackout the other night, in this instance I want to tell them all the truth, that there was no conscious desire of heroism on my part, nor was there any purposeful craziness. I had a job to do and I did it. But since everyone seems to be so eager to believe otherwise, I decide to simply accept that while I might be a potential washout as a writer I'm turning into one hell of an elevator man.

The afternoon before Moving Day, Milt gives us a speech. "Gentlemen... and lady," he acknowledges Weez with a purposeful nod. "Tomorrow we're going to be moving four hundred and twenty-two patients. We start the move at 7 a.m., which means you all have to be here at 3:30 in the morning."

I look at my watch. It's six in the evening.

"Go home, get some sleep. Lay off the booze tonight," he adds, his gaze lingering in my direction with these words.

Before we leave Milt calls D-Man and me aside. "You two are our elevator guys tomorrow. We've only got two running, which means you've got to be on top of things. This is a big gig. CNN will be here, newspapers will be here, a lot of people will be watching. I'm counting on you two guys. Tomorrow, it's *game on.*"

We nod. Milt slaps us each on the shoulder.

"Hey, Milt." I ask. "What floor is the new psych ward on?"

"Fourth, I think. Why?"

"Am I going to be taking people to that floor?" I ask excitedly, picturing haggard pop stars and sitcom actors, as well as other relatively less harmless, more amusing types.

Milt laughs. "No, Shawn. Psych patients are going to be transferred earlier. Besides, if they caught a look at you on the elevator, they'd pull you right off and admit you."

After getting home that night I immediately pour a strong drink with hopes it'll help me fall right to sleep. But as I raise the glass to my lips an alien

thought invades me: *put it in the fridge
for later.*

After I do this, I set my alarm clock
and lay down. As keyed up as I am for
tomorrow, sleep is out of the question.
But maybe a good solid rest, and then
that stiff concoction, and *then* two hours
sleep.

I'm amazed when my alarm clock is
beeping almost immediately. For the first
time in years, I apparently managed to
slip into unconsciousness without several cocktails to ease the fall.

Though three in the morning is F.
Scott Fitzgerald's proclaimed time for
the dark night of the soul, I leap out
of bed like one accustomed to the hour.
Riding my bike through the chilly pre-
morning cold only serves to invigorate
me further.

The early hours at the loading dock
pass in a blur of gondolas and reds before
D-Man and I are called to duty. We're
stationed at two elevators on the first
floor and in addition to our usual walkie-
talkies we're also issued facemasks and
gloves. When I ask him if we need to wear
them all the time, Milt answers, "No.
They're for just in case." Before he's
able to advise us on what exactly entails
an *in case,* our walkie-talkies crackle to
life: "First wave, incoming!"

Moving Day is on.

Patients begin arriving on stretchers. My first wave is mothers and their newborn babies. Proud papas accompany doctors on the elevator as we ride up to the fifth floor, the Neonatal Care Unit. The babies' very smallness lends them a precious quality, no matter if some of them seem a tad on the shriveled prune side of the looks department. Seeing the pride on the fathers' faces, the calm manner of all the mothers (probably the result of some considerable chemical sedation, but still) and the perfect innocence of these freshly delivered creatures, the inherent horror that's always accompanied the idea of having a child of my own slips away. I even begin to experience pangs of regret that I had a vasectomy five years ago.

These regrets are dashed with the second round of patients. Each of these people are surrounded by five or six doctors, one of whom is pressing a bubble apparatus every couple seconds just to keep the body on the stretcher alive. They're headed to the sixth floor, Intensive Care Unit. This is the floor, one doctor informs me later in the day, "where most patients don't even last a month." Monthlies, they're called. Many of these "monthlies" have holes in their necks or noses, and are surrounded by a web of penetrative tubes and computers that seem meaningless given how near a final breath these beings who were once young appear to be.

How can a parent bring a baby into a world that only promises death? The answer, I determine, is strength, a characteristic that has always intimidated me. Not only in others, but in myself. All my life, I've always been uneasy whenever people treat me as if I know what the hell I'm talking about.

About two hours into the day a stretcher comes wheeling up and I'm startled to recognize the homeless person I encountered on that lost evening a week ago, when I awoke in the gutter. Though his hair is slightly longer and his face seems to have gained a few more lines, I instantly peg him as my peanut savior. Bette Davis had it right when she was quoted in the Lexington, Kentucky *Herald-Leader* as saying that when you're lying in the gutter, you see people a little clearer.

He identifies me as well. "Brother!" he calls out. His voice is weak, but he manages a full smile as the two doctors on either side of his stretcher whisk him onto the elevator. I hit the eighth floor button automatically, figuring him for a liver transplant.

One of the doctors coughs. "No, we're actually going to the fourth floor."

The psych ward? I look to my friend, and he gives an enthusiastic nod. "Yeah, that's right, I'm crazy." he laughs easily, then turns to one of the doctors, a woman who seems too young, too innocent to be a psychiatrist. "Ain't that right, doc?" he asks her.

"Whatever you say, Red," she smiles back at him.

Red settles his gaze on me. "How you doin' today, young'n? How's that road you're on?"

"It's alright," I say cautiously, alternating my gaze between the lights of the ascending floors and his eyes that seem way too vibrant. What the hell is a guy who's this alive doing in a mental hospital?

"No regrets?"

I laugh. "Tons. How about you?"

He hums as if in deep thought. I try to stop recalling how Milt described his delay in answering the psycho who asked about the birds and the bees when they were trapped in an elevator together.

The bell *dings.* Fourth floor. Psych ward. As the doors open I demand of Red, "Well? Any regrets?" His hesitancy has made the answer important to me.

"None at all," he declares. The two doctors wheel him out and as the doors begin to close he calls out, "Well, maybe just one…!"

He's cackling with laughter while the doors seal shut. I want to stop the elevator, press the emergency button and pry the doors open manually. This impulse is as sudden as it is baffling. Why is it so important for me to discover this man's lone regret? Because he's able to laugh in the face of madness? Because he seems to bear no ill will toward those who judge him mad? Or maybe just because he was fearless enough to offer some peanuts to a drunken sod waking up in the gutter?

No matter. I can't leave this elevator, not now. I've got responsibilities. I've got to get back downstairs to meet the next patient coming through. Besides, I tell myself calmly while my heartbeat gradually recedes in relation to the elevator's descent, I can always go back later. Hit the fourth floor, find Red, and learn his sole regret.

However, as the day dreams on, each time my finger hovers before the fourth floor button I can't bring myself to press it. I have a suspicious fear that I'll receive a shock.

Then, as abruptly as it began, Moving Day ends. My walkie-talkie crackles: *"Final patient delivered. Everyone back to the dock."*

"You all should be proud of yourselves," Milt announces to us, once we're all assembled. We've finished moving four hundred and twenty-two patients in under five hours. The Collared Guys tell us that this was the easiest Moving Day they've ever been a part of. Milt calls me and D-Man aside, slips us sixty dollars and tells us to take our fellow temps out for a good time. He also informs us to look out for a little something extra in our paychecks. "I told you at the beginning I would take care of guys that hustle. Well, you two hustled more than anyone else. Good job, men."

So D-Man and I gather up the whole gang and head off to a local college watering hole. There we buy pitcher after pitcher of beer and talk about our lives. Many of my Delta Delta Tau brethren graduated from U.C.L.A. a month ago, and are going on to regular day jobs.

"What about you, Poet?" D-Man, who's moving to Oakland in a few days to begin a career as a financial analyst, asks me.

I sip my beer. "Keep writing, I guess."

Jamster, whose real name I've finally learned is Vincent, asks me what I'm going to write about. He's set to take a job in Chicago as an assistant to the assistant of the Public Relations Manager of the Bears.

"Life," I offer. Judging by the expectant stares surrounding me, this topic leaves something to be desired.

"Drinking!" I shout, raising my glass of beer. This elicits excited clamor from all. We toast and swallow heartily.

"Death," I add, as we lower our glasses. It's an afterthought, really.

But it's enough of an afterthought to gain Weez' attention. "What did you say?" she asks me.

Being that this is the first time she's actually spoken to me, I feel compelled to offer some kind of reply.

"It's like when I was in that elevator today, taking people up and down," I explain. "Some were going to a new life, others to death. There I was, totally insulated from the outside world, and yet I had a purpose. That to me has always been what paradise would be like. Being protected from the world's troubles while still being able to affect people. It's like writing, only… only I'm better at running an elevator than I am at writing."

This brings a laugh, which wasn't at all what I was going for. Still I can't help but smile.

"Poet," D-Man says dryly.

As the party breaks up, I shake hands with these people, all of them around ten years my junior, ready to embark on paths of their lives. I have the feeling I'm ready to embark on a path as well. But damned if I know what it is.

As I give Joseph a hug, he whispers to me, "I know you lied about the girl from that Saturday night."

I pull back. "I don't know what—"

"She's my sister."

I grapple for a response, and come up with "Uhhhh…"

"I introduced her to you, don't you remember?"

I shake my head. "Sorry, man," I say. "I don't."

He sighs and studies me so intently I start to become nervous. Here I've lied blatantly and bragged about eating underwear off his sister's crotch when all that probably really happened was she gave me a polite kiss on the cheek and directions to the nearest bus stop at Wilshire and Westwood.

Joseph pulls out a slip of paper and hands it to me. "When I told her that crazy story you made up about the two of you she started laughing. She wanted me to give you her number."

I take the slip of paper. "Why didn't you tell me I was full of shit back when I told everyone that nonsense?"

Joseph shrugs. "It was a good story," he says. "Poet," he adds, then bids me farewell.

Crazy desire grips me for the second time that day. Confess. Confess to at least one of my fellow workers, one of my Delta Delta Tau brothers, that I lied about that night in order to put forth events that, while entertaining to hear about, never remotely occurred. I want to reveal to someone just how full of shit I'd been, and most likely still am.

But by this time everyone's gone, so instead of chasing someone down to bare my soul I choose the path of least resistance. I climb on my bike and begin to pedal home. The sun is setting and I look back at Westwood and remember the first afternoon I spent on the U.C.L.A. campus. I lay on a grassy knoll amongst those halls of promised learning, and never had the world seemed so full of potential, of stories begging to be told. On that day the sun's husky red shadow had seemed to swell even as it dropped from sight, and I made a vow that I would make a difference in people's lives through my stories. The sun's lingering glow seemed a promise of glories to come. As I look back now, that same glow is there. Only now it offers a glimpse not of my future but of another's elusive past.

The next morning I snap awake at 6:15, check the Dow Jones and see that it's set to open down about two hundred points. A couple weeks ago, this news would've sent me into a fury, but now all I do is sit down and reflect on the past couple

weeks, in which it seems I've experienced a unique approval and respect never
before earned in my life. In the past
people have cheered me, chanted my supposed name, and laughed at my antics.
But these past couple weeks, especially
yesterday in the elevator, were satisfying in that I felt safe, ensconced in a
situation that was not all about me, but
about helping others.

I leaf through the pile of clothes at
the foot of my bed and pull out one of
my HCR t-shirts, the logo placed neatly
above the spot that covers the wearer's
heart. I slowly pull it over my head. For
all the deliberation I employ I could be
strapping on a Hazmat suit. Or a tuxedo.
A King's robe.

T-shirt on, I step into the bathroom
where I spend a long time staring at
myself in the mirror. Abruptly I slam my
forehead into the mirror and look back at
my reflection. There's a tingling in my
forehead but no mark on the skin. Nothing else has changed. Nobody gives a damn
whether I'm alive or dead.

I decide it's a good day for a ride. I
get on my bike and head over to U.C.L.A.
After locking my bike up at my usual
parking meter, I head inside the freshly
opened medical center's loading docks.
The easy familiar way security guards and
other assorted staff smile at me provide

a distinct comfort. I return their greetings and confidently head over to one of the elevators.

My first passengers are a pair of doctors. "You guys were awesome yesterday!" they both say to me and my HCR t-shirt. As the day moves on, I encounter many doctors I met the day before. All treat me with an admiration I find intoxicating. Whenever one of them asks me where the rest of the team is, I explain that they're doing cleanup at the old hospital. Everyone's so accepting of this bit of fiction that I almost grow to believe it myself throughout the day, even though I know that my coworkers won't be back and all the Collared Guys are already on their way back to Canada.

The next day when asked about the whereabouts of my coworkers, I calmly assure all that "they're around" and that we'll most likely be here a couple more days to finish off paperwork and consolidate things. Once again, there's much laughter and banter in the elevator as I push buttons and shuttle doctors and patients from floor to floor.

By the end of the week, doctors are giving me curious looks when they board the elevator and see me there. "Are you still here?" they ask. One in particular, a woman with short red hair who introduces herself as Dr. Kaplan, seems especially interested in me. She asks several questions about who I am, and I answer to the best of my ability. The truth is I'm not all that sure. I don't feel like a writer anymore, I don't feel like someone who needs to care about the stock market or the latest stimulus plan. An even more staggering change is that for the past week I haven't had one drink. All I feel I need are these four walls of my elevator and a fresh supply of people coming on board who need to be taken somewhere. I have a purpose, even if it only lasts for a few floors.

After I leave the hospital at 5:30 Friday evening, I don't go back to my apartment. Instead I lay down on the grassy slope in the center of campus, the same place I'd perched when I first dreamed of attending this school in hopes of becoming something. I don't move as the sun sinks into the west, those final few seconds so much faster than one might expect. Time passes, and in the darkness I can hear the hoots of students as they make their way across the main walk. Their shadows so animated in the moonlight. I find myself both envying and pitying of such energy. I was that young once, I think, and remorse and relief intertwine.

I spend the entire weekend on U.C.L.A. grounds, buying perfectly satisfactory meals from the campus taco stand for just three dollars a day. The cashiers smile at me as I pay for my one chicken soft taco at a time, which I go to eat in the Franklin D. Murphy Statue Garden among various erotic and thought-provoking works sculpted from bronze and stone. At nights I sleep beneath fat palm trees.

I fall asleep easily on Sunday night, looking forward to tomorrow morning when I will go back to work.

Next thing I know there's a light shining in my face. I blink and try to swat it away. "Hey, buddy," a gruff voice says. "You can't sleep out here."

I blink my eyes several times and am finally able to make out a campus security guard. "What the hell are you doing here?" he asks. "Too much to drink and had to pass out?"

The irony of this shocks me. I realize, with exhilarated trepidation, that I haven't had one drink for a solid week. This is the longest I've been sober since I arrived in Los Angeles.

I hold my arms up to shoulder's length. No shakes. I look around and don't spy any rodents scurrying anywhere. There are none of the symptoms all those anti-drinking Public Service Announcement films warn you about delirium tremens.

I start to laugh. "Amazing!" I exclaim.

"All right, pal," he says. "You're coming with me."

The guard goes to grab me but I shake away and flee, scrambling out of the bushes and down a small concrete path that weaves around the media center complex. The guard's shouts fade as I meet up with the main walk that connects the campus to the outside world. The medical center is only half a block away. I fly down the sidewalk and duck into a back entrance I know is always open.

Once inside, I check a clock and see that it's 4:22 in the morning. Minutes away from the time I awoke in a gutter back when what seems like a million years ago. I head over to the elevators and press the button for mine. Once inside, I curl up in the corner, my knees pressed against my chest. The doors close, and I close my eyes, secure in the knowledge that when somebody needs a ride they will open.

Ding!

At the sound of the elevator reaching a destined floor, I leap to my feet. When the doors split apart I see Dr. Kaplan. She smiles at me, her lips a shade lighter than her auburn hair. "Do you want to come with me, Shawn?" she asks.

Because she has asked me a question, given me a choice of surrender instead of a demand for it, I am able to accept.

I haven't kept track of how long I've been in here. Of course there are sessions with doctors, pills I'm given to take (which I don't), and group meetings with other people who are referred to as patients. I've looked for Red, but nobody seems to have any memory of him. According to the doctors, there's no way I could've brought him up to the fourth floor on moving day. "We got all the crazies in here early," one doctor told me when I asked. "No offense," he added quickly.

I assured him, honestly, that none was taken.

I've realized I wasn't lying that day on the loading docks, when I told Joseph about why I wrote. It's a matter of trying to play a small part in a scheme that is as dazzling as it is inexplicable. Here, I have the freedom to share my stories with others on the fourth floor while also learning theirs. I'm also allowed to ride the elevators, and thus have the power to take passengers to life-affirming moments such as visiting a newborn as well as the inevitable farewell to a dying loved one. I am a perfect link in an imperfect chain, taking people where they need to go.

I remain forever young, secure in my role here as the poet in the elevator, that's all. For what else is a poet but one with the courage to admit that they and the world around them are, in the end, a work in progress.

SPECIAL FEATURES - THE LOST POEMS

Note: If DVDs can have "Special Features," then why not books? These were amongst the mass of poems found in Shawn Michals' apartment after the time of his disappearance. Many of them (such as the first three featured in their original form) were partially burned, as if thrown into a fire and then recovered. Maybe Shawn didn't want the world to see them. However, he was the one foolish enough to put me down as an emergency contact, and I have a suspicion he believed I would be foolish enough to try to get at least a few of them published. Though there were many, I have, after countless hours spent sorting through and doing my best to interpret his scrawl, chosen a few to have transcribed in this book that will hopefully convey various extremes of his life in Los Angeles and how he viewed his fellow inhabitants.

- B.P.

Splinters ~~of thoughts~~ melting into
~~thoughts~~ sq~~ueezed~~ to dust
~~coming~~ a poetic laughter ~~mixing with a sense of~~
these grains of sand drop from sight
loved by ~~those~~ ones afraid of being alone
leaves of b~~oth~~ chances not taken
~~blooming with~~ ~~joy~~ ~~and~~ ignorant repulsion
The beat of ~~the~~ ~~hearts~~ stolen from another world
~~by who crafts~~ their hearts to embrace
a baby's cry
fighting mightily against the darkness
of a life which will forever be unknown.

~~Shaves~~ of light Protest all
against petals of bloom leading into you so
there is no end You will

~~The night~~
The dawn will come, Rest assured that the sun will rise
again. But there will be ~~times~~ of darkness
stretching across the corner of the ~~night~~
Broken down into minutes
which chill your blood
~~Fo~~r as you sit in bed drinking quietly
& staring at the ~~door~~ ~~eyes wide with tears~~
You shudder, pulling the blanket closer for-
useless warmth. Raise the glass for another
drink which makes the seconds go faster
And you ~~have~~ had enough of these nights & know
that you will count every one of them
losing yourself & stare at the blood
leaking from the small windows in your room
And there seconds keep coming and there's not
a damn thing you can do.

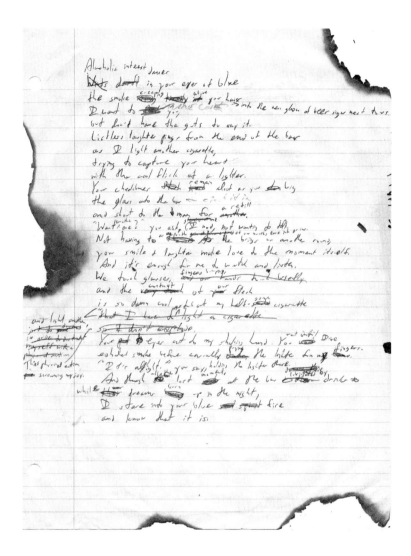

AN ANGEL ON EVERY CORNER

A friend once mentioned a country song
with a chorus that suggested homeless people
who begged on corners
may in fact be angels in disguise
sent down to test our generosity.

My response was that to believe this
would make slums the place where one
could find angels on every corner
many times two or three
gripping paper bags filled with fuel for
their wings.

Encouraged by his smile I went on
about the ones who hold up signs reading
WILL WORK FOR FOOD
Should these particular "angels"
be considered potential traitors
seduced by the thought of obtaining the cars
they see passing them every day
are they ready to fall
turn in their wings for a three piece suit
their brown bagged elixir for a cellphone
that would drop them into the cluster of
human greed?
Are these figures marked with scabs and
the reek of unwashed flesh sent by God to
test the human race?
Maybe not, my friend admitted.

Damn right, I nodded.
In this world, the one we live in
homeless people
are simply homeless
the mad, the dispossessed, the ones who
don't fit in
who have no power to either take or issue
bribes
castaways and castoffs
from a society in which currency is used to
measure not only success
but generosity of its-

I stopped, caught.
In other words
my friend nodded along with me
Angels.

SAFE

He sat in his car
stopped dead on the freeway
a lighter in one hand
the collar of his only friend in the other

an angry line of cars gathered behind him
their horns demanding a move
one he sought as conclusion

not just to the tape he'd recorded the
previous night
his cat at his side
accepting his confession
as she'd accepted all about him

but to a life that had been too much his own
the difference in him that had grown
shaped into worms by his mind
that believed he had been born sick
diseased with unacceptable desire

the virus inside of him a seeming vindi-
cation of
his family's long worn scorn
a scarf tightening

now with the stench of gasoline
giving him a mild high
he sparked the lighter
and the ease with which the motion came
left greasy dots of joy on his sheet of despair

that he would never see the day when it
would be a struggle to even move
the horns behind him now a chorus of cheers
his last thought as he set his body on fire
was of his cat at home
the video he'd posted on YouTube
a self-shot plea for someone to adopt
his cat
someone good, caring
who wouldn't mind that she
was shy and unlike most cats
not especially independent,
afraid of being alone and unable to meow,
only purr

the flames cut off thought
went to battle the waiting worms
so eager to consume him

while in the room that had once been his home
a cat with no collar paced
alone, frightened,
safe

DYING IN PARADISE

Sitting at a table in a restaurant or bar
in L.A.
(said the casual one)
Many of the waiters and waitresses have
grand dreams of
(said the observant one)
being famous, being wealthy… being a Star.
(said the cynical one)
I enjoy talking to these people, and tip
them well.
(said the secure one)
It's fun for a true genius like myself
(said the delusional one)
who has pretty much given up any dreams
of blinding fame
(said the lying one)
to see people so bent on achieving their
fantasies.
(said the condescending one)
But I try not to go back to the same restaurant or bar
(said the cowardly one)
too may times, for more often than not I
find the same
(said the analytical one)
people there… still talking about audi-
tions, etc.
(said the world-weary one)
their eyes shining with hope rooted in a
reality
(said the whimsical one)

that is still unfulfilled.
(said the told-you-so one)
I wonder what they think about as they
make their way
(said the curious one)
to and from work every day, take crap
from customers,
(said the pitying one)
and see teasing images of sound-stages
and premiers
(said the smartass one)
amongst the burgers and fries and shakes
on their trays.
(said the hungry one)
Perhaps a few will make it
(said the hopeful one)
But more of them won't.
(said the knowing one)

I know I just have
(said the grateful one)
in the time it may take to read this poem.
(said the grasping one)
I'll live forever
(said the prophetic one)
within those seconds
(said the dying one)

Now, would you like a drink before dinner?

I love you, Mom.

About the Author

This is Ben Peller's second novel. He is currently living and drinking as much as he possibly can, and no doubt hoping you will join him when he comes to a tavern near you.

Editor's Note:

Shawn Michals was last seen in the psychiatric ward of a medical center in Los Angeles. His current whereabouts are unknown.